GOD

A BEGINNER'S GUIDE

GOD

A BEGINNER'S GUIDE

CAROLINE OGDEN

Hodder & Stoughton
A MEMBER OF THE HODDER HEADLINE GROUP

Orders: please contact Bookpoint Ltd, 39 Milton Park, Abingdon, Oxon OX14 4TD. Telephone: (44) 01235 827720, Fax: (44) 01235 400454. Lines are open from 9.00–6.00, Monday to Saturday, with a 24-hour message answering service. Email address: orders@bookpoint.co.uk

British Library Cataloguing in Publication Data
A catalogue record for this title is available from The British Library

ISBN 0 340 78080 0

First published 2000
Impression number   10 9 8 7 6 5 4 3 2 1
Year   2005 2004 2003 2002 2001 2000

Cartoons by Richard Chapman
Typeset by Transet Limited, Coventry, England.
Printed in Great Britain for Hodder & Stoughton Educational, a division of Hodder Headline Plc, 338 Euston Road, London NW1 3BH by Cox & Wyman, Reading, Berks

Dedication

This book is dedicated with love to the memory of my father, John Nelson Ogden.

I am indebted to Mr Andrew Clutterbuck, Senior Lecturer in Study of Religion and to Mr John Lippitt, Senior Lecturer in Philosophy, both at the University of Hertfordshire, for much of my inspiration for whatever may be considered good in the book.

CONTENTS

Contents

PREFACE

This book does not aim to give the reader a detailed account of every religious viewpoint or even of every viewpoint within the religions on which it touches. It is a Beginner's Guide and it is hoped that the reader will wish to explore further within his or her chosen subject areas.

It also does not aim to inspire the reader to religious belief. The author has a firm faith, but hopes that this is not apparent within the text, as it is most important that this be impartial and academically rigorous. The author favours what is known as the phenomenological approach, which involves a going inside the subject area and making one's account of it as if from that viewpoint. Nevertheless, she is aware that there may be some objective comments on particular religions which, simply because they must be objective, will not be viewed favourably by their adherents. She apologises for any offence which may be caused thereby.

With that, the author wishes the reader 'God speed'.

Does God Exist?

For as far back as we can go, humanity has always felt the need to worship something or someone greater than itself. Most people would agree that this is instinctive, even if not everyone agrees that it is justifiable. People have constructed reasoned arguments for the existence of this being, which we shall call God, and these would seem the best starting point in any exploration of the nature of God, humanity's experience of Him, how belief in God relates to other aspects of man's life and problems that arise from that belief.

Note: Although much modern thinking supports the use of pronouns other than the masculine applied to God (as we shall see in Chapter 10), for simplicity and clarity we shall retain the traditional masculine form (with a capital H) in this book, along with the generic masculine applied to humanity.

Arguments for God's existence come from many different grounds. There is the **circular argument**, that 'God must exist, because one look at His universe shows that He is all-powerful and all-loving'. It will be obvious that, no matter how strongly felt, this argument takes as its evidence the very thing it has yet to prove! Equally, to argue from the existence of a **moral sense** would be to assume a moral nature to God, which is again to assume His existence. Others refuse to use logical conventions. The general definition of 'faith' even suggests that logical proofs cannot be used, or faith is destroyed. We will nevertheless look in detail at two of the oldest formally set out types of proof for the existence of God – the ontological argument of the influential Christian theologian St Anselm (1033–1109) and the cosmological argument of the philosopher and theologian Thomas Aquinas (1225–1274).

KEYWORDS

Circular argument: argument that uses as a proof the very thing it is trying to prove.

Moral sense: the capacity to distinguish virtue from vice; the admiration felt for good acts; one part of the reasoning faculty of man.

ST ANSELM'S ONTOLOGICAL ARGUMENT

The meaning of the word 'ontological' has to do with the nature of being. The **ontological argument** for the existence of God attempts proof by analysing the concept of God. It is known as an *a priori* proof, meaning 'prior to experience', i.e. rational or by reason alone (as opposed to empirical or *a posteriori*, meaning 'after experience'). This means that it takes God as a given and then tries to demonstrate His nature, rather than arguing that nature from what is seen.

In the first part of the argument, Anselm refers to the atheist who says 'God does not exist' and argues that, in order to deny God, the atheist must first have had a concept of God to deny: Anselm described God as 'that than which no greater can be conceived' but if the atheist then denies the existence of Anselm's conception, he must first agree that definition, which means he must have 'God' in his mind.

> **KEYWORDS**
>
> Ontological argument: attempt to prove God's existence through analysis of the nature of the concept of God.
>
> *a priori*: based on reason alone; not provable empirically.
>
> *a posteriori*: based on reasoning from facts or particulars back to the general, from effects to their causes; inductive.

Anselm goes on to explain that, for something to be 'that than which no greater can be conceived', it must exist in reality as well as in the mind or understanding, since to exist in both is greater than to exist in the mind alone. Therefore, if the atheist has 'God' in his mind, God must also be in reality. Otherwise, the atheist is conceiving of something, the definition of which he has agreed, yet at the same time denying that definition. And the definition itself would be false, since God would exist in the mind (of the atheist) but not in reality and therefore could not be 'that than which no greater can be conceived'!

Anselm went on to state that God could not be conceived not to exist, for a being that can be thought not to exist is not as great as one that *cannot* be thought not to exist. In other words, existence is necessary to the idea of God.

This argument is circular, certainly, but it is known as a **formally valid** argument, meaning that neither the premises (or steps) of the argument nor its conclusion need to be true as long as the conclusion can be seen to logically follow from the premises. But Anselm was not trying to prove God's existence to non-believers. He accepted that faith was a means of understanding and his argument merely set out to demonstrate that those without this faith were in error in denying God and that this could be proved logically. Much of the problem in these arguments for the modern mind arises from the idea current during Anselm's time of the concept being identical with the object, so that 'to have a thing in mind' was meant rather more literally than we might realize!

KEYWORDS

Formally valid: valid by being perfect in its form; even if the arguments are not true, they cannot help but lead to the conclusion.

Cosmological Argument: argument for God's existence from the existence of caused things.

Coherence theory of truth: a statement is true if it fits with other statements or another outlook on the world.

Correspondence theory of truth: a statement is true if it fits with the way the world obviously is.

Anselm's argument belongs to what is known as the **coherence theory of truth**, i.e. something is true if it fits, or coheres, with the system (of belief or language etc.) in which it is found.

GAUNILO'S REPLY

Anselm's argument was challenged by a contemporary, the monk Gaunilo, who argued that we often describe fictitious things without their actually existing and yet other people are able to understand that they are fictitious. He used the example of an imaginary island, perfect in every way and therefore the greatest that could be imagined, and said that it did not follow from this (a) that it actually existed, just because it was possible to have it in mind or (b) that the idea was any less perfect because it did not exist in reality.

ST THOMAS AQUINAS'S COSMOLOGICAL ARGUMENT

In his **cosmological argument** Aquinas sought to demonstrate God's existence not because he considered it non-self-evident, but because he realized it was not a self-evident conclusion for ordinary people to draw from their experience. His arguments for God's existence belong to the **correspondence theory of truth**, i.e. something is true if it corresponds to observable, objective reality. Aquinas's argument is from the observable world and works from the effect back to the cause. He believed it was not possible to argue in the other direction since we could not presume to understand God's nature or essence. His is thus an *a posteriori* (empirical argument). It is laid out as five proofs:

1 The Argument from Motion

Everything is in motion. Anything that is moved must be moved by something. The act of movement means that something changes from being in a state of potentiality ('on the way') to being in a state of actuality ('arriving'). Only something already in an actual state could make this happen, just as only fire can make something actually hot, because it is itself actually hot. This 'mover' cannot be the same as the thing which it moves, as something cannot be simultaneously potential and actual. Nor can this 'mover' itself be moved by something else, or again it would not be actual. So it is known as the First Mover unmoved by anything before it, i.e. God.

2 The Argument from the Nature of Efficient Cause

Everything has an efficient cause of its being. Nothing can cause itself, or it would have to exist before itself. There may be a whole chain of effects, each of which causes the next one, but the first effect has a cause with no cause or effect before it. This is known as the First Efficient Cause, i.e. God.

3 The Argument from Possibility and Necessity

Everything in existence in nature – or the 'created world' – has the possibility, in fact the potential, to be or not be, e.g. everything alive now will *not be* so at a set point in the future. Things now existing as seeds have the potential to *be* plants, animals etc. But anything with the potential to be cannot be in existence at all times, and anything with the potential not to be must at some time equally *not have been*.

Therefore, everything must *not have been* once, but in that case nothing could have come into being, which it obviously did, and so to avoid the problem of **infinite regress** already met in Arguments 1 and 2 (i.e. going back and back *ad absurdum*) there must be something whose existence is necessary to everything else, but which was never in a state of not-being and which has its own necessity, i.e. God.

KEYWORDS

Infinite regress: the situation of a chain of events or effects going back to infinity without a first event or cause in the chain, where everything starts.

Teleological: argues from the apparent purpose behind the world, the seeming goal or completion of everything.

4 The Argument from Gradation

This argument was later taken up by the French philosopher and scientist Renée Descartes (1596–1650), who said that, for us to recognize imperfection, there must be perfection to measure it against. Aquinas said that in nature some things are more good and true etc. and some less. However, to make these comparisons implies a maximum (or superlative) to compare them against, just as we say something is hotter the closer it comes to the absolute state of being hot (the 'actual' we talked about in Argument 1). Aquinas then quotes the fourth-century BC Greek philosopher Aristotle, who said if there is something that is great*est* or tru*est*, in other words the absolute best, it is also the greatest in being and if the maximum in any class is also the cause of everything that can be said to be within that particular class, as again the maximum of heat is fire and this is the cause of all hot things (we now know this to be the energy generated by friction, but the argument still stands), so there must be something that is the cause of every quality it has and that is shared by nature, including the state of being itself i.e. God.

5 The Argument from Governance of the World

This is also an 'argument from design' (see page 6) and is **teleological** in nature, meaning to do with goals, purposes, completion etc. Aquinas argues that everything acts for a purpose, even things without thought of their own. This is evident because these things always, or nearly always, act in the same way and for the best. This cannot be due to chance but to design. If things without thought can act according to a design, it must be that something over and above them is directing them with that design in mind, i.e. God.

We can see from these proofs of Aquinas that he makes many assumptions. His arguments are circular, in that he presupposes the type of God he is arguing for and structures his arguments to fit that image. Also, many people do not believe in the necessity of a prime anything - but in spontaneous generation of life etc. and even in the possibility of infinite regress which Aquinas could not accept, e.g. 'no one created the world, the Big Bang was generated by energy/expansion/contraction etc.'

THE ARGUMENT FROM DESIGN

The cosmological argument of Aquinas is not the only type of *a posteriori* (empirical) 'proof' (any more than the ontological argument is the only type of *a priori* (based on reason) proof. The English theologian and philosopher William Paley (1743–1805) sought, at a time when man was discovering the wonders of mechanics, to prove God's existence by likening this world and the universe to the workings of a watch. From the wonders of this intricate mechanism we must infer the existence of the watchmaker for, even when the watch occasionally goes wrong, this does not disprove the design and intention. In answer to the infinite regress problem, even if the watch could be proved to have come from a previous watch, there would still have to have been a watch originated by the watchmaker in the first place and any generation from watch to watch would only prove his genius further. The Scottish philosopher and historian David Hume (1711–1776) criticized this argument by saying that:

✳ the analogies between the universe and such a mechanical item as a watch were inaccurate and we would be better off likening it to something of animal or vegetable nature.

* the greater mind responsible for the world (the watchmaker) did not need explanation, when the physical existence of the world it had supposedly made did.

* the order in the universe could have come about randomly over time.

* the inference of a wise, potent and kind being from his creation is questionable in that we might infer as much from any human invention to its inventor but be very disappointed on meeting the actual man.

Many see creation as working like clockwork

KANT'S MORAL IMPERATIVE

Many of these proofs have much to say about the nature of God and thus this chapter will overlap with the next to some extent. Our next *a priori* proof from the German philosopher Immanuel Kant (1724–1804) is one of these. He does not argue that God exists in a way we can know or prove, but says that because reality affects man as an ethical being as well as a rational one, man's practical reason believes (rather than knowing intellectually, as does his theoretical reason). Kant argued that:

* theoretical reason has its limits and that one must deny knowledge, in order to make room for faith;

* practical reason accepts certain metaphysical facts, such as freedom, immortality and God's existence, all of which are proved by the very operation of that practical or moral reason.

Kant's argument was that there is a 'highest good', which was not only virtue (or morality), but virtue crowned with happiness. In other words it is not enough if a man is a good being if he is not happy too. From this he argues God's existence by saying that in nature we would not achieve this just apportionment of goodness and happiness, so there must be a guarantee of who is above the laws of nature. So the existence of God is assumed as a necessary condition for our realizing the goal of morality, i.e. the higest good. God and morality are inextricable.

THEOLOGICAL REJECTION OF PROOF

The Bible makes no attempt to prove God – for the authors this did not even enter into question. They experienced God directly and did not have to infer His existence. Many religious faiths teach that God gives free will and therefore the choice to believe or not is man's. For God to prove His own existence would take away that choice. **Fideism** takes the philosophical position that proofs are not valid, but this does not negate God's existence, as faith has nothing to do with reason but with religious experience. Danish philosopher Søren Kierkegaard (1813–1855) and contemporary British theologian John Hick (1922–) are two more recent apologists for this view, but the earlier French philosopher, mathematician and physicist Blaise Pascal (1623–1662), said 'the heart has reasons which reason knows not of'

KEYWORD

Fideism: the doctrine that religious truth is a matter of faith and cannot be proved by reason.

(Pensees 1670). He is known for 'Pascal's wager', which (although it uses a form of philosophical reasoning) would be regarded as based on faith alone. It argues that, since no proof is available for God's existence, it makes more sense to believe and be rewarded with Heaven if one's belief turns out to be true (while one loses nothing if it does not) than not to believe and risk damnation if one turns out to be wrong.

This completes our brief look at arguments for God's existence, some of which make certain assumptions about the nature of this God, which we will examine in greater detail in the next two chapters.

✳ ✳ ✳ ✳ SUMMARY ✳ ✳ ✳ ✳

- Many arguments for God's existence are circular.

- Anselm argued for God's existence from His nature, but from reason rather than observation.

- Aquinas argued for God's existence from His nature, but as deduced from the observable world, with five proofs.

- Kant argued for God's existence from morality.

- Faith is destroyed by proofs and is considered to have more validity because it is given freely without them.

2 Who is God? Immanence, Transcendence and Form

If He exists, what is He like? We have already seen that some of the arguments for His existence use assumptions about His nature as part of their proof. These assumptions are essentially that He is all-loving, all-powerful, all-knowing, the First Mover who has existed eternally and could not be conceived not to exist.

There are also attributes, such as **transcendence** (i.e. being completely unknowable and unreachable) or **immanence** (i.e. being everywhere and in all things). These views affect how He is worshipped, the relationship man feels he has with Him, what kind of precepts or morals or ethics His adherents follow. They even influence the design of places built for His worship. And, of course, they affect man's understanding of good and evil and what may happen after death.

KEYWORDS

Transcendence: an attribute of God which makes Him above and separate from the material world, beyond the reach or understanding of humanity.

Immanence: the quality of being present in all things, so that they are imbued with the divine.

HOW RELIGIONS REFLECT OUR VIEW OF GOD

Before we look at how specific religions view God's nature and identity, let us explore in a more general way just how aspects of religious life are affected by which views of God are held. If we say God is transcendent, we immediately suggest it is hard to have a relationship with Him or to understand as much about Him. This may leave us in awe, but possibly feeling alone and insignificant and uncomforted. If we say He is immanent, then we do not recognize so much of His majesty – and His omnipresence and thus omniscience are put in question. This may seem a paradox when we are saying He is everywhere in all things, but being 'in' all things might not necessarily imply the same degree of omniscience as that which views from a height and sees everything simultaneously and clearly.

Where places of worship are concerned, we see in the Jewish temple and in the Christian Roman Catholic, Orthodox and Anglican Churches a great emphasis placed on the altar, the place where only the priest may approach, symbolizing the holiness of God. Here the

KEYWORD

Mediator: one who acts between others, particularly where reconciliation is needed.

priest is the **mediator**, the link between transcendence and immanence, for God, who is unlimited and out of time and space, can be said to be present in this place for His people. In the same way the Host, or communion bread and wine, symbolizes or *is* (depending on whether you are Protestant or Roman Catholic respectively) God Himself present in His creation (matter) and in the partakers' souls, in the person of Jesus Christ.

In Islam, however, God may not be represented and nothing living or man-made may be bowed to, no matter how symbolically. While this would seem to suggest even less chance of approaching God, since a

The style of building (or altar) may express much about a particular traditions concept of God.

physical medium tends to ease our path as material beings, it also puts the relationship on a more direct footing, in that no one and nothing else may mediate between God and His servant. Here God's transcendence is not seen as a barrier to a personal relationship. Equally, many Protestant and non-Conformist Christian churches have dispensed with the priest as mediator, and with the altar and other objects as symbols of the divine (which are often in danger of being mistaken for the true object of worship), seeing Jesus Christ as the only mediator needed and the relationship with God as a direct one. Here there is often far less ritual also.

Where God's other attributes are concerned, His all-knowingness, all-powerfulness and all-goodness become very relevant when considering the problems of evil and morality (we will look at this in Chapters 6 and 7). Theories of life after death are also coloured by whether one believes in a personal God (e.g. Will we retain our personality and individuality and meet loved ones again?), a forgiving God (e.g. Will we attain Heaven? What is Hell like?) or a knowing God (e.g. Will we be able to hide from Him what we have done?)

As far as life here is concerned, the type of God people believe in colours the type of person they strive to be. Christians talk of God or Jesus Christ being 'in' them and they 'in' Him, while Jews see God as instrumental in their history and politics, because they are His 'chosen people' who follow a strict code of laws given personally to their patriarch Moses by God. Both faiths see God as entering into personal **covenants** with them and personally giving them rules for life.

KEYWORD

Covenants: binding agreements, especially involving promises from God to man.

PLATO'S FORMS

Important to our exploration of God's nature are some of the views of philosophy. The influences on both Christianity and Sufism (a mystical sect of Islam), for example, came not only from the Semitic tradition but that of the Greek philosophers Plato and Aristotle. Plato is best known for his philosophy of 'Forms' or **universals**. This explained how we may find meaning in a word applied to more than one thing. For example, every tree can be called 'tree', suggesting that somewhere exists the archetype of that quality or essence of 'treeness' that makes it a tree, which we might call 'tree'. This is not just a question of logic but of **metaphysics**, for this **archetype** is also an ideal in which its lower manifestation, or **particular**, participates imperfectly. As British philosopher and mathematician Bertrand Russell (1872–1970) said, using a cat analogy, the archetype is *the* cat, which is created by God and is unique. The particular cats, i.e. all the cats in the world, partake of *the* cat's nature, but they do this more or less imperfectly. This is why it is possible for there to be so many of them, because *the* cat is the actual reality and its particulars, the earthly cats, are merely apparent.

KEYWORDS

Universals: absolutes, archetypes, the origins or models, their individual realizations or particulars.

Metaphysics: to do with ultimate reality, the abstract, the non-material and the transcendent.

Archetype: the original or prototype of a thing, its perfect example.

Particular: the individual, material realization of a universal.

Apprehension: a direct experience or understanding of something through the reason or other means than earthly sight, for Plato a kind of recognition.

So, 'the Good', 'beauty' or 'tree' are the archetypes or 'universals' of each independent example of goodness, beauty or tree, and we recognize these universals when we name their instances here, because we have a dim memory of an existence before this one.

By necessity, of course, these universals exceed their earthly instances – they are ultimate, and only they have true reality, which we know by a direct **apprehension**. All their particulars (their instances here) are mere appearances/opinions, knowable by the senses. Many religions have rejected this world as unreal and see eternity as ultimate and having the only reality. The universals of goodness, justice, truth etc. are held up as the ideals to attain to and thus ascribed to God by many religions. Their universal nature means they remain unchanged, another attribute of God we have already encountered. Plato however actually identified God only with the Form of the Good, which he said gave existence to all other Forms.

We can see immediately the relevance of all this to ethical considerations as well as in describing God – and how these two are linked. The Jewish and Christian idea of man being made in the image of God makes God the universal, and man shares (imperfectly) in His nature. This means, where ethics are concerned, that because universals of qualities such as goodness, justice, truth etc. are eternal and perfect, so necessarily their particulars here share only imperfectly in their qualities – and so man strives to attain the perfection of the universal qualities.

ARISTOTLE'S 'FORM'

Aristotle however saw no division between the realm of the senses and the realm of 'ultimate reality'. He believed something was real if it could be perceived by our senses and the universal of a thing for him was its form here, rather than its Form! Form equalled function, which was part of a thing's identity. So, for Aristotle, qualities and virtues were less unattainable than for Plato. Although Plato did see the Forms also as a guiding principle and nourishment to the soul, resulting in its longing for completeness, full of being and knowing everything, for Aristotle an abstract idea is necessarily unattainable and does not work even as a guide. He said that even if there was one Good which was universally predicable of (i.e. you could say it about) all goods here, and was capable of separate and independent existence from them, clearly this could not be achieved or attained by man.

Since Aristotle's 'forms' were actual and here – 'enmattered', i.e. consisting of matter – he believed they were attainable. Where, for Plato, a quality existed universally as a separate entity, for Aristotle it was a property of a particular man with no separate objective existence and by nature was defined only by being done and by the way in which it was done. So an act was tied to the person acting and, by definition, one could not perform a good act unless the whole of one was good (or, to put it another way, the act could not truly be called good unless the person acting was truly good). This avoids the idea of good as a separate entity that one may tap into in spite of oneself, and is reflected in the way that Islam and some schools of Christianity emphasize personal responsibility. Plato's idea, however, was that direct apprehension of the Forms does lead to right action, and we can see this reflected also in St Augustine's succinct saying: 'Love and do as you like'. Plato's idea of the world as having no ultimate reality can be seen in a happy synthesis with Aristotle's opposite view (of form in this world equalling man's fulfilment of his purpose, which is excellence) in the philosophy of the Jesuit priest and writer Teilhard de Chardin (1881–1955). He wrote about the *pleroma* the fulfilment of creation, a completion of God's purpose, being worked at by man through ethical behaviour. St Augustine talks also of 'the realm of becoming' and 'the realm of true being'.

Now we have established the importance of Greek philosophy to the three 'religions of the book' (as Islam refers to Judaism, Christianity and Islam) we will proceed to look at these and other religions' ideas of God in more detail, taking advantage purely for considerations of chapter length (and not with any other emphasis intended) of the convenient division into 'pre- and post-Christian'.

✱ ✱ ✱ ✱*SUMMARY* ✱ ✱ ✱ ✱

● God's transcendence or immanence affects the way man relates to Him as well as affecting forms and places of worship.

● Mediation reconciles transcendence and immanence, but is often seen as an obstacle to a closer relationship with God.

● Plato suggested an ultimate archetype or universal for everything which he called a Form. God is the Form of the Good.

● This has ethical implications, whether because man's moral behaviour is improved by his apprehension of the Forms, or because he is condemned to be unable to achieve the Good, as it is not of this world.

● Aristotle believed in the forms as enmattered, a part of the material world and the function and identity of all things.

3 Who is God? The Religious Experience of Man (pre-Christian)

The Greeks inspired not only Christianity and Islam but Judaism and the earlier Roman culture, and the latter in turn also influenced Eastern Orthodox Christianity. Any order in which we look at individual religions risks a loss of emphasis on one of these connections and so we will try to cover them instead according to a vaguely chronological listing of the forms in which we now know each of them. We will, however, make the exception of placing Judaism before Christianity rather than at the head of the list, because of the intimate nature of the relationship between the two. We must unfortunately limit ourselves to what may be termed 'world religions', which means omitting many religions of great interest which are termed primitive or minority (in terms of world influence although not of numbers).

HINDUISM

Hinduism emphasizes God's immanence and this is seen in the abundance of gods illustrating the many faces of God the unknown, as He interacts with mankind. As in Christianity, there is also the idea of mediation expressed through the belief in the **incarnation** of God as man in **avatars** such as Krsna (or Krishna) one of the most popular Hindu gods.

Hinduism began as a **polytheistic** religion of nature worship, involving sacrifices for which

the Rig Veda was the accompanying hymn-book. By the eighth century BC, thinkers who opposed such practices claimed to know by direct intuitive insight the supreme and universal principle of being and collected together in the *Upanishads*, a body of work reflecting in many different forms the same perceived essential truths. This was eventually incorporated into the official system by means of a fourfold scheme of life prescribed for Brahmin (the priestly class in the Hindu caste system), which concentrated on freeing the self from the illusion of self, culminating in an inner knowledge of divine reality and the union of *atman* (the personal soul or self) with Brahman, the infinite, all-pervading ultimate reality and soul of the universe, who is the self in all and the stuff of which the world is made. This union is expressed in the phrase *tat tvam asi* ('thou art That'). Thus there is paradoxically a sense of divine transcendence but also of divine indwelling and, as with Plato, a belief in something else that is a higher reality, while all else is *maya* (illusion or ignorance). This is not a personal God, as is the God of 'the people of the Book' (Jews, Christians and Muslims) and as were the gods of the Romans and Greeks.

However, this is only one form of developed Hinduism, expressed for example in **Advaita Vedanta** (the way of non-dualism) and which dates from the eighth or ninth century AD, where man's relationship to the divine is that of a seeking to return to the fire from which he came by freeing himself from matter and desire and the illusion of self through knowledge. A later form is that of **Dvaita Vedanta**, a **dualistic monotheistic** belief that we are fragments of the divine who should glow as brightly as the fire we come from, with the emphasis on our relationship to that Ultimate through right action to overcome our bonded situation. However, the material world is considered real and sacred and our 'bondedness' to it means we must act *in* it. Desire and self are here seen as dangerous only if uncontrolled and undirected. We can see from this how important

KEYWORDS

Advaita Vedanta: Hindu term for non-dualism – the idea that all is one, matter is spiritual and there is no division.

Dvaita Vedant: Doctrine of dualism in Hindu thought.

Dualistic: the division of the world and human nature into matter and spirit, resulting often in a perception of good and evil as equally matched.

Monotheistic: believing in one God.

is not only the perception of God's nature, but also the perception of creation, to an understanding of man's relationship to God.

Shiva, the Hindu Lord of the Dance.

In Hinduism, time is **cyclical** and therefore there is less emphasis on an act of creation, as this is something believed to be happening repeatedly. Hindu myths say something important about the Hindu perception of man's relationship to God and also, as with all creation myths, help to explain some of man's failings. In one **monistic** 'emergence' myth (note the sense in this word of something gradual and less of one particular event in time), the power of warmth causes matter to exist, which in turn causes desire which is

the germ of Spirit. Here there is no creator and all diversity is in fact one, with one constitution. A second example of the emergence myth still has the Absolute imbuing the created order and the ultimate Reality as something other than matter, but man is here a fragment of the Absolute, which ordains man's social structure and system of action, while matter is not illusion but sacred and eternal, with man's goal being to work for the ordering of the cosmos. These two myths give very different explanations for man's problems and failings. The first attributes them to a lack of recognition of man's being one with the Absolute, where any sense of self involves desire and desire is error. This is the Advaita Vedanta. The second attributes them to the *wrong* desires and actions of the self hindering the work for cosmic harmony. This is the Dvaita Vedanta.

BUDDHISM

Buddhism developed out of Hinduism from the life and works of Siddhartha Gautama, a sixth-century BC prince. Buddha means 'the enlightened one'. As with Hinduism, it teaches the cause and effect chain of **karma** and a path whereby man can cease to suffer. It also teaches that it is desire and the sense of self-identity that are responsible for man's unhappiness. However, its essential difference is that it does not accept the Vedic philosophy of a change-less and permanent Reality and therefore does not accept the idea of God. It is in fact **anti-realist** about self or Plato's universals. The German philosopher Friedrich Nietzsche (1844–1900) saw Buddhism along with Christianity as **nihilistic**, in that both denied any ultimate difference of value between one man and another (but he saw Buddhism as the less objectionable of the two!).

> ## KEYWORDS
>
> **Karma:** the law of cause and effect governing human existence, in which one's deeds determine one's destiny.
>
> **Anti-realist:** denying that something is independent of the mind, saying it does not have an independent existence or reality outside our thought.
>
> **Nihilistic:** believing in nothing (from *nihil* meaning 'nothing').

It may seem strange that a religion that denies all reality to this world and to the self (even the redeeming reality of their being imbued with the Absolute, or being mere imperfect realizations of it, or being at peace by attaining union with it) can nevertheless preach an ethical code. However, Buddha was known for his great love of humanity and advocated following the **Eightfold Path** of ethics to enlightenment and peace.

Many religions preach that knowledge or recognition of the divine and consideration of questions about mortality and eternity are necessary to an understanding of right ethical behaviour and to salvation, but Buddha insisted that such metaphysical questions merely distract one from the goal and that a person who insisted that they be answered before they follow the path to enlightenment would be like a person wounded by a poisoned arrow, who will not let the surgeon remove the arrow until they have found out all about who had shot it, etc.

KEYWORDS

Eightfold Path: Buddhist system of spiritual training that leads to deliverance from suffering.

Reincarnation: being reborn in different forms, for spiritual improvement.

Nirvana: bliss, the ultimate state of blessedness, involving loss of self and a freeing from reincarnation.

However, there can be no doubt that the Buddha's experience was a religious one (although as intellectual as it was mystical). He wished to discern the ultimate reality of things and although this resulted in his assertion that there was no ultimate reality, he still saw a goal of existence and a morality that determined man's spiritual journey (i.e. either continuous **reincarnation** or the attainment of **nirvana**). His lack of belief in God resulted partly from his preoccupation with and compassion for the suffering of living beings, but we may suggest that the term 'God' may be interpreted in different ways. The Buddha's impatience with man's concern over 'who shot the arrow' is also because the questions are wrongly put and they do not help in the path through life.

Despite the absence of God, Buddhism does contain its own mythological gods, but they are part of the cosmos and thus impermanent and subject to the same karma and with the same striving for nirvana. In the Mahayana branch of Buddhism, an emphasis on the division between the impermanent and the transcendent gives Buddha a transcendent role, above these gods, justifying such beliefs by the Buddha's own claim that nirvana is indescribable. It is, of course, human nature to ascribe to the inexplicable, the ineffable, a quality of divinity. This the Mahayana describe as the 'unconditioned', as opposed to the belief in the Theravada school of Buddhism in the conditioned and impermanent. In this way, Buddha himself becomes a part of that transcendence and there is a tendency, despite his teaching, to worship him as divine, rather than honour him as human.

JUDAISM

Judaism in its present form began in the thirteenth century BC with Moses, who brought to his wandering people a strict code of laws and a belief in one God. Until this time, despite later attempts by Jewish writers to edit the earlier scriptures in order to backdate monotheistic belief to those times, this belief was not prevalent and the ancient Hebrew tribes were polytheistic and **pantheistic**. Like Christianity, Judaism places great importance on historical events because of what they say about man's relationship with God and about the character

> **KEYWORDS**
>
> Pantheistic: believing in God as immanent in the material world in a very intimate way, so that all natural phenomena are manifestations of Him, e.g. thunderstorms are signs of His anger, rain of His tears.
>
> Polytheism: belief in several gods.

of a God who concerns Himself with this world. The strict code of the Commandments forms part of a covenant with God, whereby He will look with favour on His people, if they abide by His rules. This was a very new idea: a personal relationship of responsibility to one God. This God was not even to a superior God over many lesser gods, as, although it may have started like this, the resultant ascription of less power to God meant the eventual rejection of **polytheism**. It is likely that the strong Israelite prescription against succumbing to the temptations of polytheistic religions encountered in their wanderings had instinctively political motives. The covenant with God was part of the ethos and identity of the Chosen People to which they could cling in their tribulations. Nations and groups of individuals in exile inevitably come together in an assertion of cultural and ethnic identity. Thus the

Jews, like the Muslims after them, have strictures about the worshipping – or even the making – of images. However, symbolism is a human need and part of human worship and in Solomon's temple, God was given a physical 'resting place' in the Ark of the Covenant.

The success of monotheism for this people, who constantly found themselves wandering or colonized and thus in contact with many other religions, rests with their political aspirations – in turn strengthened by their constant experience of being dominated by other powers. Their prophets' words were important as much for the political, earthly progress of the people as for their spiritual progress, since keeping the covenant ensured their status and their good fortune as God's chosen ones. Political events were interpreted in the light of God's will. Prophets were intermediaries between this transcendent God and His people, experiencing His awesome power in the form of great lights, burning bushes, even blindness and dumbness, as proofs of that power. Holiness could only exist in ethical action, because the sense of sin in the face of this majesty is so great. It was this focus on 'the law' that led Jesus to condemn the establishment Jews of his day as followers of 'the letter and not the spirit'. Its importance also lay firmly in this life rather than the next, whereas for Christianity, which is based on Judaism, the one leads to the other.

In the Jewish creation myth of Genesis, God creates all matter out of nothing. This means that without God, man and the universe could not have existed and this not only makes them utterly dependent on Him but, by setting His action in time, establishes Him as a part of the history of man and the universe, as is demonstrated throughout Jewish scriptures. The dependence on God involves obedience and it was man's self-assertion and presumption that caused him to sin.

Just as the Garden of Eden had an identifiably historical setting, so would man's future ideal existence, perceived as a restoration to the Jews of their nation and their land – in later belief to be effected by a Messiah, an anointed of God who would combine the spiritual and the physical salvation of His people. These ideas necessitated a view of evil as a power in opposition to God and of suffering as lack of harmony with God's will. The omnipotence of God is retained through the idea that God allows this evil for His own purposes and we will look further at this belief in Chapters 6 and 7.

✳ ✳ ✳ ✳SUMMARY ✳ ✳ ✳ ✳

- Hinduism lays emphasis on God's immanence.

- Advaita Vedanta is non-dualistic, i.e. does not divide the spiritual and the material, so man is seen as seeking to return to union with the divine, through loss of desire and self-identity.

- Dvaita Vedanta is dualistic, i.e. divides the material and the spiritual, so man is seen as coming from the divine but as acting within a sacred material world, where desire and self-identity are not wrong *per se*, but only if uncontrolled.

- Buddhism does not believe in a divine being and considers such questions distracting.

- Judaism is a monotheistic and legalistic religion putting forward belief in a personal and historical God who has entered into a covenant with His chosen people.

4 Who is God? The Religious Experience of Man (post-Christian)

At the risk of appearing to give more attention to Christianity than to other world religions, we will later divide this section into the three main branches of Eastern Orthodox, Roman Catholic and Protestant, excusing ourselves with the justification that, although the basic concept of God is the same in these branches, they differ greatly on the nature of His relationship with man and man's path to redemption in ways that have impacted considerably not only on Christians but on world history, because of their relationship with different power structures.

CHRISTIANITY

Christianity derives from Judaism. Its leader was born a Jew and its first adherents were Jews. But where, for Jews, the Word of God is the Scriptures, for Christians the Word is the person of Jesus Christ. Christianity, like

Buddhism, has always been a proselytizing (aiming to convert others) religion and spread rapidly to Gentile areas. It preaches the consummation of the Jewish history of God's relationship with His chosen people in the coming of the Messiah, but extends the definition of 'chosen' to all those who accept the faith that the Messiah has come and has the power to offer spiritual **redemption** and a new relationship with God. This new covenant is evidenced not by the rainbow of Noah or by the Ten Commandments of Moses, but by the crucifixion of the same Messiah in a blood atonement for the sin of man. However, although universal, the redemption is dependent in turn on man's belief in this Messiah. This point became crucial later in the differing emphases on salvation, by faith or by works, of the later Roman Catholic and Protestant Churches. The link between Judaism and

Christianity is seen in the Apostle Paul's references to an old and a new Adam, one symbolizing fallen mankind and the other being Christ, both man and God: 'as in Adam all die, so in Christ shall all be made alive' (I Corinthians 15, 22) The old order was upturned and God and man were reconciled. Life now meant a spiritual existence here on earth and entailed continuance after death. Life without Christ was death.

The belief in Jesus as the Messiah posed problems. If divine, how did this square with monotheism and a belief in God's omnipotence? If human, how did this symbolize God's covenant and the significance of His intervening in the affairs of men, to suffer at their hands? The history of the early Christian

KEYWORD

Dogma: belief set out as official by a sect, group, or party, acceptance of which is obligatory for membership.

Churches is littered with accusations of heresy and the convening of meetings to establish **dogma** in the face of doubt and dissension. The Eastern and Western Churches have never succeeded in being unified on many of these points. Their differences were inevitable also because of the difference in culture, politics and language.

Eastern Orthodoxy

The Council of Nicea (an assembly of bishops convened for the maintenance of doctrine and discipline) in AD 325 ruled that the problem was solved by God and Jesus, with the Holy Spirit, being 'one substance' but three persons, so that the divinity of God was not diluted in any way by making a separate Christ equal to Him and yet that divinity could still be attributed to Christ. However, this was later revised for the benefit of the Eastern Church, because it did not sufficiently express the different persons of God and Christ. Later yet, in AD 451, the related question of how Christ could embody both divinity and mortality was answered by describing these aspects as different natures of the person of Christ.

Images were another source of conflict between East and West, as within the early Jewish faith. The Eastern Church used **icons**, stylized representations, which they came to revere as means of prayer and a path to God

– aids to contemplation, in other words. This was seen by the Church of Rome as idolatry (for which it was itself condemned by Protestant Churches).

Mysticism in orthodoxy includes the tradition of 'Peace', which through repetition of a particular prayer, aims at the mystic communion of the soul with God, involving visions of and union with the light of God – as opposed to His essence, which is unknowable and to claim union with which would be blasphemy. Church

services have a repetitive and slow quality which induces a sense of the mystic and otherworldly.

Roman Catholicism

Like the Orthodox Church, the Roman Catholic Church has a hierarchy and ritual, which symbolizes the delegation of authority by Christ to His disciples, from the chief of whom, Peter, all bishops (and thus all priests through ordination by those bishops) are said to be in direct line. For the Roman Catholic Church, this establishes their authority over Eastern Orthodoxy, as this unbroken line cannot be claimed by the latter, and results in the Roman Catholic belief in the infallibility of the Pope. Central to both Churches, however, is the **Eucharist**, the re-enactment of the Last Supper of Christ with His disciples, where the bread and wine stand for the body and blood of Christ, God's sacrifice of Himself for men's sins and a means of spiritual refreshment by, and communion with, the divine. The Roman Catholic Church believes that this bread and wine are not mere symbols, as the Protestants believe, but in some mystical way through the operation of God's grace become the actual substance of Christ's body and blood, thus meaning God's actual coming again into the physical world.

Another point of belief in which the Roman Catholic and Protestant Churches differ is related to belief in the incarnation of God as man.

For Catholics this *is* the body and blood of Christ; for Protestants, it represents them.

The Christian doctrine of the virginity of Christ's earthly mother, Mary, derives from the belief that Christ's divine status means the seed from which He grew must have been divine not human. However, the Roman Catholic Church extends this to a belief that Mary, in order to have been worthy of bearing God, must also have been born of a virgin and not of the seed of man. It can easily be seen that this must necessitate an infinite regress (of the kind we saw in Chapter 1 objected to by Aquinas in his proofs for God's existence), for one must then say the same of Mary's mother, and so on. The Protestant objection to this is that it implies a perfection in Mary akin to Christ's and perfection is a state only attributable to divinity. It also nullifies the power and significance of God's gesture in becoming man if He is seen to be born not from mankind but from a semi-divine being.

Protestantism

The Protestant movement sprang out of an objection to the political power of and corruption within the Roman Catholic Church and to what it saw as an undue focus on works and on physical representations, while losing sight of the direct relationship to God through faith in Christ which the Apostle Paul taught. The old idea of sin and the granting of salvation by a stern God to those who did good works was rejected. Forgiveness was a gift and all that was necessary was (right) belief. This doctrine became known as justification by faith. The movement developed to trim away everything that did not seem to have the authority of Christ Himself or His disciples and Apostles, especially Paul. One marked aspect was making available to all God's Word (and thus Christ, the true Word) in the translation of the Bible from Latin into the vernacular. Mediation is done away with in many ways in this Church, thus empowering ordinary people.

The tendency however was to replace the old authority of the Church with the new authority of the Bible and a rigidity developed which forbade any diversion from Biblical doctrine and emphasized man's low status without

KEYWORD

Predestined: decided before time; fated.

God's grace (or gifts). The first part of Romans 3.24, 'All have sinned and come short of the glory of God', inevitably came to have more emphasis than the second 'being justified freely by his grace through the redemption that is in Jesus Christ'. But the French reformer and theologian John Calvin (1509–1564) developed the further doctrine that God chose who should be saved by faith and who not. This was thus **predestined** and good works again came to the fore, not as a means to salvation, but as a mark or sign of it.

ISLAM

Islam, meaning peace or harmony by submission to God's will, was founded by Muhammud the Prophet in the sixth century AD, after a direct revelation to him by God (Allah) of the *Qur'an* or *Koran* (meaning 'Recital'), which he wrote down despite being illiterate, as it was revealed to him during a series of ecstatic visions. This is the only miracle claimed in Islam. The Qur'an is the infallible word of God, as Christ is to Christians, but Islam's crucial point of departure from Christianity is that it sees belief in the incarnation of God in Christ as blasphemy. Allah is transcendent: supreme, unknowable, unchangeable – and One. He thus cannot be represented in any way by humans. Man is separate from Him and, although having a spiritual side, is not in any way 'made in His image' (whether metaphorically or otherwise) as Jews and Christians would say. The Christian belief in the division of the substance of God into three persons is seen as blasphemy because it implies not only polytheism, but the coupling of God with a human and the lessening of His supremacy. Man has responsibility and stewardship over the earth and God is merciful and compassionate, so that Adam's sin, born of free will (although this became less and less emphasized) and the influence of the fallen angel Iblis (the Lucifer of Judaeo-Christian belief), is not one inherited by all mankind but was forgiven him at the time it was committed, although God is seen as predestining some to damnation. Iblis is not a power in any way equal to God, his ability to obstruct God's work being limited by God Himself.

As with the other religions 'of the Book', Islam follows a set of laws or guidelines, to which its followers must adhere to do God's will. These religious duties, known to Islam as the **Five Pillars**, involve prayer, fasting for the purifica-

> **KEYWORD**
>
> Five Pillars: the five religious duties of all Muslims.

tion and focusing of body and spirit, almsgiving, pilgrimage to Muhammud's birthplace, Mecca, and repetition of their creed that 'there is no God but Allah and Muhammud is His Prophet'. The ethical duties involve right attitude (thus avoiding an empty following of God's laws when not for the right reason, i.e. love of God), fairness, compassion and there are taboos on gambling, alcohol and eating pork.

Muhammud established not only a religion of personal faith, but one by which a strong political community could be created. Muhammud is believed by Muslims to be the last and greatest in a line of prophets sent by God to His people, which includes the Jewish prophets and Jesus Christ. God's mercy lies in His teaching to men via the prophets, His power and glory directly experienced by these men in a mystic ecstasy. The words of the Qur'an are said to have the power in themselves, because direct from God, to inspire and convert.

Islam, like all religions, has been subject to division, the main one being that between the Shi'ites and Sunni Muslims. The Shi'ites hold a messianic belief that centres on the descendants of the Caliph (chief defender of Islamic faith) Ali. Despite Islams being opposed to the persecution it witnessed in Christianity, orthodox Muslims repressed Shi'ites for political and economic as much as religious reasons. One result was the belief by Shi'ites that God's revelation was now confined solely to their own Imams (religious leaders).

This branch contributed to Islamic mysticism, which grew out of an interpretation of Muhammud's experience as largely mystical rather than prophetic and a rejection of the exterior forms of the Islamic religion which, as in Christ's condemnation of Judaism, was seen as having lost sight of the Spiritual. Sufi mysticism was objected to by orthodoxy, because it seemed to emphasize a mystical relationship with God as immanent, at the expense of an awareness of His transcendence, and thus suggested that man, by being united with Him, took on an element of the divine. Neo-Platonism provided a compromise, through the idea of man having his Form, or eternal prototype or ideal, contained within the nature of God, so that the direct experience of God in a mystical encounter was man meeting up with his own prototype. Just as Plato's knowledge or direct apprehension of Good (or God) resulted automatically in virtuous action, so did that of the Sufi mystics, although not so much automatically as through the love it inspired in them. Sufism was a seeking for the Permanent by those entrapped in matter and the things of this world, the *maya* or 'illusion' of Hinduism and Plato, which have their opposites in the permanence of Plato's Forms or the Judaeo-Christian ultimate reality of God over the created world, amongst others.

＊＊＊＊SUMMARY ＊＊＊＊

- Christianity is regarded by Christians as the fulfilment of Judaism and is based on the belief that the promised Messiah has come.

- Jesus is regarded as God, but God is still seen as 'the one God'.

- Eastern Orthodoxy and Roman Catholicism are the Eastern and Western branches of the original Christian Church.

- The Eucharist, the celebration of the Last Supper, is viewed differently by Catholics and Protestants – the former believing the bread and wine become the body and blood of Christ, the latter believing they symbolize them.

- Salvation by faith was a major principle of the Protestant Church.

- The Protestant Church emphasizes the Bible as the Word of God, with greater authority than the Church.

- Islam regards Judaism and Christianity as having a flawed understanding of God's word and believes it has the final revelation.

5 What do we Mean by God? Language, Myth and Symbol

It is easy to see how many different things may be meant by God, despite definitions that seem to be common to all, such as 'something divine', 'a power', 'ultimate reality' (and even these may be differently defined!). In addition, for those who do not believe in God, or who may believe in qualities of God different from any encountered in religious language, there is a major problem. Should they even use the word 'God', if others will understand by it something different from what is intended, or is it a useful starting point and the only way of introducing something on a level understood by all? In Chapter 1, we saw that Anselm said that when someone claims they don't believe in God, they must be accepting the concept (and therefore its existence), in order to reject it. But just what concept is expressed by this word, when such variety of ideas exists as we have seen in the last chapter? In this chapter, we will glance at what philosophy and linguistics have had to say about this problem and will also consider how myth and symbol appear to be common to man's religious language and to fulfil a human need and how those that are culture-specific may still express universal truths.

In philosophy, an argument is considered 'valid' even if its propositions (i.e. its content or steps) are false, providing it follows a correct logical form. Therefore, many philosophers without belief in God might still accept Aquinas's proofs for His existence as valid. But philosophers such as John Locke (1632–1704) would argue, following the correspondence theory of truth, that a word may not describe something abstract, but only a particular thing, in a one-on-one relationship to it. Proof would then be required of the existence of that thing, in order for the word to have that relationship.

MYTH

The theory of structuralism followed by the French anthropologist Claude Lévi-Strauss (b. 1908) suggests myth is a special form of language and looks at the relationship between the elements of a myth (or of a language) as they are in the present moment, rather than over time. There is no point in trying to pick apart the individual elements. One might apply this to talk of God by saying it is no use asking what we mean by 'God'; this will be revealed if we see what is being said, if we look at the whole story, just as we understand a game of chess by looking at the board and how all the pieces stand in relationship to each other, rather than by finding out about the history of the game. This idea has strong echoes of the later philosophy of Ludwig Wittgenstein (1889–1951). We have already encountered the correspondence and coherence theories of truth (see Chapter 1), terms used to describe respectively the situation of truth fitting with the way the world is observed to be or of truth fitting with the outlook within which it is expressed. Wittgenstein originally adhered to the former in his 'picture

The Word of God is mediated through the scriptures and interpretation is a constant problem.

theory of meaning', where the relationship between words in a sentence (i.e. its structure) corresponded to the relationship between things in the world which they described, and where religious language could not be part of

language proper. In his later philosophy, he argued the coherence view that the meaning of a word lay in the way in which it was used and what was intended by its user. This went against Anselm's argument of a word or concept, if used, implying the existence of the thing to which it refers, and Plato's and Parmenides's idea that even if something is thought not to exist, it must do so as a Form for us to be able to speak of it. But it gave scope for acceptance of any concept or word. Terms did not need explanation or justification – they were understandable in context or in that 'form of life' in which they were uttered. (Aquinas, of course, would have argued that everything is in God's context, since all was created by Him, and this is why there is no problem!) As well as involving tolerance for different types of language use, this view must also lead to tolerance for different cultures' expressions of what God is and means for them. **Linguistics** also has developed a branch called 'pragmatics' which looks at how we use and understand language beyond its obvious sense.

The word 'myth' is often taken to mean something untrue. *Myth* is in fact Greek for 'word', but meaning a word that is presented to elucidate and inform, like a window onto another world or sense of being. Man cannot do without it or without symbolic language in general judging from it's universal presence. Its function is to work out, if not to solve, problems and questions, with its terms not so much applying to things as acting as a living dynamic in man's understanding. It may also be used to legitimize a particular culture or custom, with gods emerging to represent the particular interests of that society. The French sociologist Émile Durkheim (1858–1917) even suggested that God was society's projection of itself, with collective self-enhancing rituals acquiring sacredness and then being objectified into the worship of a supreme being. If we go back and apply much of this to the last two chapters, we will see how it works, with creation myths generally legitimizing man's place in the order of things or explaining the presence of sin, or a flood myth emphasizing the favourite status of a particular race, i.e. the Jews. We also see that myth does not imply lack of truth, although men may disagree about the details of that truth, and truth may be seen to be a relative rather than an objective reality. However, most societies believe in the objective truth of God in whatever form.

SYMBOL

Many religions, even those that forbid the representation of God, use imagery to express things about Him and man's relationship to Him. Light and darkness are widely used to differentiate between good and evil or knowledge and ignorance – hence God is often seen as light or fire. Morning is a symbol for hope and new beginnings, and the rainbow for God's covenant with man.

Human language is able to deal with terms on two levels, so that a word may have its ordinary linguistic reference and also its religious reference. When we consider that all words are in fact symbols for that to which they refer, it is not hard to accept their extended meaning also. Words are often considered to have great power – sometimes superstitiously so in certain cultures. 'The pen is mightier than the sword' is at least as popular a saying as 'sticks and stones may break my bones, but words will never hurt me'. A symbol such as the poppy may instantly evoke a whole world of associations, and the word 'poppy' may be understood as implying all that too. In Christianity, bread and wine symbolise something other than the literal. In many religions, the very name of God is considered to have power, if invoked.

So, in using symbols, in writing poetry, in using religious language, and in performing religious rituals, we are trying to express something over and above what these words and actions may mean in our everyday world. We may be said to be stepping onto another plane, into another time and place that are sacred. Linguistics contains theories about words being performative, i.e. having the power to effect something by their utterance alone. The Polish anthropologist Bronislaw Malinowski (1884–1942) held similar views. But it has been argued that religious language is not about reality but about commitment to a particular way of seeing and set of values or attitudes, so that praying for something does not have the intention of persuading God or of changing the order of things, but is an assertion of the attitude of the person praying, e.g. in the Christian Lord's Prayer, 'Thy will be done on earth' meaning not 'may everyone conform to Your will' but rather 'I accept your will'.

Wittgenstein said that the world of the happy man was different from the world of the unhappy man, although the facts of that world were the same for both. Man's faith colours his view of life and his language. In the next chapter, we will see how those with faith have formulated arguments to justify aspects of the world which to the unhappy man and the man without faith seem unjustifiable.

✳ ✳ ✳ ✳SUMMARY ✳ ✳ ✳ ✳

● Some philosophers have argued against religious language and proofs for God's existence, saying that language must describe a reality in a one-to-one relationship with it and that proof of the thing's existence is therefore required before we can speak of it.

● Myth is not necessarily a lie but a perceived truth, using a particular form of language appropriate to its context.

● Myth functions as a form of therapy, social legitimization and explanation and is usually culture-specific.

● Symbols enable man to express the inexpressible and may have great power.

Problems of Reconciliation: Evil and Death

Possibly the most frequently asked question in relation to religion is about the problem of evil and suffering. The question can take two forms, either questioning God's nature (e.g. 'How could God be good and yet allow this to happen?') or His existence (e.g. 'If there were a God at all, He would not allow this to happen'). These two questions have been answered by various versions of what are known as **theodicies** and we will look at these later. First, we will give a brief outline of some views on and explanations of evil, as well as

KEYWORDS

Theodicy: a justification of the existence of evil by the citing of arguments such as the free will defence or the soul-making value of evil.

The Fall: Man's original sin, and the permanent state of sinfulness resulting from this for all of mankind.

looking at related worries about death, which as well as being seen as a consummation and reward, is also often feared as the unknown, or resented as unfair. This in turn relates to the problem of reconciling spiritual beliefs and aspirations with love of the material world and reluctance to leave or renounce it. We will then examine how religions have used God's name to commit acts that seem opposed to what they preach as His word. Finally we will look at theodicies which attempt to explain some or all of the above.

EVIL

Evil is variously defined, from the mere absence of good to the presence of a power equal and or necessary to that of God, and may describe both actions and their results, or events and their results. It may be seen as something that man cannot help – e.g. in the Judaeo-Christian idea of **the Fall** – and/or as something he deliberately chooses through ignorance or wilfulness, but could avoid. It can be seen as something that inevitably pervades anything **temporal** and material, or as something that has been introduced to the temporal (by man, gods or angels) and corrupted it. It may be regarded as mere illusion, not really existing, as for example with the Christian Science view of disease being an error of the mind.

KEYWORD

Temporal: literally 'of time', but implying earthly, an opposition of things spiritual.

As we have seen, most creation myths attempt explanations of the nature and presence of evil and at the same time of why death is at the end of man's earthly existence. The Judaeo-Christian story of the Fall is twofold, describing the fall of Lucifer, God's highest angel, and the fall of mankind when tempted by him. The common thread is a pride which puts itself above God and wishes to claim for itself the knowledge and power which are His alone. This greatest sin then becomes the heritage of all humanity and is seen as the cause of all its misfortunes and of death as the end

Does man have the right to question God at all, if he owes his existence to him?

of life. It is used to explain not only man-made problems and disasters but natural ones too, by the idea of the corruption of the natural world by the force of this sin. The Jews at one time came to see the battle between good and evil as an equal one and risked losing sight of the view of God as supreme, but this was later restored, along with the introduction of the Messianic faith that evil would eventually be vanquished in both earthly and spiritual realms. In the meantime, its presence was vindicated most vividly in the Book of Job, where God replies to Job's complaints: 'Where wast thou when I laid the foundations of the earth?' (Job 38.4) In other words, man is created by God and has no right to complain of a life that is only his by the grace of God.

We have talked about the Hindu belief in karma, which is a form of determinism but allows for the actions of the individual to work out his fate (see Chapter 3). In the non-dualist Advaita Vedanta, man's problems are seen to emanate from desire, an attachment to matter (which is illusion) and a sense of self. His only way back to union with the fire of his origin and a state of non-individuality is by freeing himself from all these, through the gaining of knowledge. However, the dualistic Dvaita Vedanta accepts the material world as man's true home and part of God's creation and concentrates on the type of desire and sense of self as being good or bad – a view somewhat akin to the Judaeo-Christian view of man being made in God's image – and suggests the end as a union with the divine that still retains individuality.

IN THE NAME OF GOD

Since religion began, man – while attempting to come to terms with the problem of evil – has used religion to justify some of the greatest acts of evil, whether justifying these in terms of the 'greater good' (i.e. the ends justify the means) or whether convinced of their rightness. It is this fact that prevents many people from accepting religion and thus accepting God, since the two are perceived as synonymous. The empiricist philosopher Ernest Nagel (1901–1985) comments on the passion with which atheists argue for their views and comments that atheism is in fact a protest against institutionalized religion as much as an actual belief about God. Of course, many believers in God respond that it is the very problem of evil that causes man to act thus against God's will and nature and that the face of religion should not be confused with that nature. For someone outside that belief, this is not always helpful. This is why there is such emphasis in Christianity, for example, on Christian witness, which is not merely about statements of belief, but about actions reflecting that belief and presenting 'the face of Christ' to the world.

But Christianity and other religions have been persuaded, through their zeal to convert, their claim to sole possession of the truth and their pursuit of whatever is perceived as morally right, to perform some appalling actions. Arguments as to whether evil is evil if its doers genuinely believe it is good begin to look like sophistry in the face of, for example, the Grand Inquisition, the persecution of witches or any number of wars where God is invoked as being 'on the side of right'.

THEODICIES

We have already said that the term 'evil' can describe actions or their results. It is also used of both natural and man-made states. The British Chritian philosopher Richard Swinburne (1934–) defines these respectively as **passive evil** and **active evil** (although we have already noted that some religions see natural evil as consequent on man's fall). It is the problem of active evil that has inspired what is probably the best known theodicy of all, the free will argument. We will look first at this and other theodicies concerning active evil and then turn to passive evil.

> **KEYWORDS**
>
> Passive evil: the results of evil, such as human suffering; also applied to evil that cannot be attributed to man's actions.
>
> Active evil: evil directly attributable to man and his Fall.

The free will argument says that there would have been no point in God creating beings who loved and obeyed because they could not do anything else. This would nullify the value of that love and obedience, which are, it is argued, by definition *freely* given. Inevitably with this freedom comes the choice between good and evil, right and wrong, kindness and cruelty, justice and injustice, selflessness or selfishness. God, therefore, in giving man free will, voluntarily gives up His right to prevent him using it. The resultant evil is still worth it, because the good has more meaning through being chosen voluntarily.

It could be argued in response to this that He might still intervene in serious situations, just as a parent might when seeing its child endangered by its own or another's actions. For however one may argue that parents should leave their children free to discover through their own mistakes, this should not be extended to allowing them free reign when it may mean serious harm to themselves or others – spiritually or physically. Many theists and theodicists would argue that God *does* intervene at times, citing reported miracles and personal experiences, or even events that may still seem evil but are said to prevent further and greater evil. Ultimately, they may bring forward the argument from Job, that while man has a duty to prevent suffering, God has rights over us which may put Him above that duty. However, just as man may gauge where and where not he needs to intervene, it is also argued that God may see how unimportant earthly suffering is in the total scheme of things, e.g. in the face of eternity, and also that there are limits to the amount of evil actions possible and thus to the amount of pain it is possible to suffer in this world.

Another theodicist argument runs that God allows evil because of the good that may come out of it . For example, the compassion shown by carers for the injured, the ministry of those called to a religious vocation, the sacrifice of life or liberty for a just cause which may inspire others. All these may be seen as higher goods for the souls of those either performing or witnessing such deeds.

Even if all these arguments are accepted where human actions are concerned, there is still the area of passive evil to discuss. When innocent human beings suffer earthquakes, volcanoes, storms, fires, floods, disease or unprecedented loss of loved ones, the question is asked 'why?' Here there is no direct human action involved that can be attributed to free will or the Fall – there is only the natural world. We have said that some beliefs extend the presence of evil or error to matter generally (i.e. the material world), and this might be seen as one explanation. Also, of course, many disasters seemingly unrelated to human error may in fact be seen otherwise – forest fires and underground station fires have been caused by litter; floods and storms may be more frequent because of changes in the atmosphere encouraged by pollution and resultant global warming; landslides and wind damage may be aggravated by the absence of trees destroyed by greed. There is also the argument of God as the great scientist who, having set the universe in motion with its mathematical laws, would almost make a mockery of the whole creation if He were continually to break in and make exceptions to His own laws. It is not argued that He cannot, but that He will not because it is illogical, and God is not illogical.

If an opponent were to point out that theists *do* however claim that God has sometimes intervened, this theodicy could still argue that that intervention may be actually a possibility written into the laws of this mathematically governed universe. It may come under the laws of chance – set up by God and therefore still His action – but not describable as a direct intervention or exception to His laws.

Of course, in the material world in which man lives, many pains (physical or mental) may be said to be necessary as safety mechanisms, to warn of the dangers of fire for example, to curtail too much self-indulgence, or to cause a man to look closely at himself or give him greater impetus to achieve something. Again, it might be argued that disasters too give mankind the opportunity to show heroism, compassion or patience and inspire him to work for ways of preventing their reoccurrence. We will see in Chapter 8 how these aspects of science may sometimes run into controversy, when it is questioned just how far man may go in 'playing God'.

In the next chapter, we will summarize by type the theodicies we have touched on here and look in detail at some arguments and objections.

✳ ✳ ✳ ✳ *SUMMARY* ✳ ✳ ✳ ✳

● Evil may affect what we believe about God's existence or about His nature.

● Active evil is that caused by man and passive evil is that suffered by man and/or caused by 'nature'.

● Man usually seeks to explain the source of evil in his creation myths.

● Religion is often made the excuse or justification for evil acts, which can have the effect of alienating outside observers from God or belief in Him.

● Theodicies are justifications put forward to defend God against accusations of cruelty or injustice, by putting things in another perspective and particularly by bringing forward the argument of free will.

7 Theodicies: Following the Arguments

THE IRENAEAN THEODICIES
Irenaeus (AD 30–200), an early theologian, put forward a positive doctrine of Christianity, arguing that God is partially responsible for evil and that:

* evil is soul-making, a test (what the Utilitarian philosopher John Stuart Mill (1806–1873) called 'constructive unhappiness' and the Jesuit preist Teilhard de Chardin justified in the idea of the *pleroma* (see Chapter 2), the fulfilment of creation where man would have worked with God to achieve this fulfilment and to become His likeness);

* evil is a man-made discord in a beautiful music, an idea which J.R.R. Tolkien developed in his creation myth in *The Silmarillion* (see Chapter 8 on subcreation);

* we would need to see from God's perspective to understand (a view to which Aquinas inclined, see Chapter 1).

The general emphasis of the Irenaean approach is less on the Fall than on man working with God towards perfection.

AUGUSTINIAN THEODICIES (AFTER ST AUGUSTINE, 4TH–5TH C. AD)
Another early, influential theologian St Augustine (AD 354–430) put forward the arguments that God is not to blame for evil, and that:

* evil is soul-deciding (i.e. man's choices for good or evil will decide his fate);

* the world was created perfect, but man misused the gift of free will and caused the Fall;

* to counter the possible objection that a perfectly created world would have no potential for evil, the free will argument is brought in.

The emphasis of the Augustinian approach is on morality as the choice between good and evil, involving freedom.

RICHARD SWINBURNE'S THEODICY

Let us now follow the steps of Richard Swinburne's theodicy (a developed synthesis of the above), to give us a clearer picture of the arguments.

Problem	*Swinburne's answer*
✳ Evil is incompatible with an all-knowing, all-powerful, all-loving God, who could and would by definition prevent it.	✳ Some evil is good, a warning, or may lead to greater goods.
✳ A perfect God could not do a morally wrong act, such as creating or permitting evil.	✳ The free will defence. It would be wrong to create people not free to do good. The value of good, free actions outweighs the evil of any opposite choices.
✳ What about the consequences to the innocent victims of an evil act? Shouldn't God make sure there are none?	✳ Without these, there could be no concept of our responsibility for each other and we would be living in a 'virtual reality' kind of world.
✳ Couldn't God at least cause only the withholding of pleasure or benefit, rather than allowing active pain?	✳ Yes, but even withholding benefits can still cause passive evil. God must let children learn from pain, to develop character and responsibility.
✳ Can man be given too much responsibility? How can evil such as Nazi concentration camps be valid?	✳ God does limit the amount of pain it is possible to bear. The degree of evil equates with the degree of resultant good and the degree of responsibility given. We need evil to enable us to do good deeds.

✳ Why couldn't evil be something we believed was happening and acted on accordingly, but without it really hurting anyone?

✳ If it is part of man's duty to stop evil, why is it not part of God's?

✳ What about natural disasters that humans do not cause but cannot prevent?

✳ That would be morally wrong.

✳ This would mean God was a deceiver, which would be morally wrong.

✳ We don't have an overall view. We can only act on what we think are probable consequences. God has rights over us anyway, which we do not have over Him.

✳ Men are still responsible because of the Fall. It nevertheless provides opportunities for good action. So God may even cause them Himself.

✳ The Irenaean idea of the soul-improving purpose of evil, enabling man to work with God. Man's anger at evil and pain gives evidence of his right thinking and care for others. The higher good is so worthwhile, it is worth asking man to suffer. God's high demands make Him worthy of our worship. Finally, in the Christian belief and in some other traditions (e.g. the Fisher King, Isis and Osiris, Demeter etc.) God shared our humanity and showed His solidarity by giving Himself in the shape of His Son to suffer also, to redeem mankind.

Some objections to the above from both sides of the argument

* You cannot liken God to a parent and say what would be right or wrong by these standards. If God does something, it is right.

* You cannot say evil gives the opportunity for good actions and responsibility – this would make others' misfortune a chance for self-righteousness.

* You cannot say that evil produces good – there is nothing noble about suffering.

* You cannot say God limits evil to what we can bear – this is to be abstract about suffering – the sufferer still suffers terribly.

* You cannot say passive or natural evil give man a reason to change things – it depends on men's characters.

Many of these objections suggest that theodicies are insensitive, that God's actions are incompatible with the concept of His goodness, and that evil is pointless and unjustifiable.

Spare the rod and spoil the child – may evil be justified as a means of improving character?

THE REVISIONIST VIEW

This approach would say it is not the job of philosophy or religion to offer any theodicies – these are rational/scientific attempts which, by likening God to man or judging Him by man's standards, misunderstand the way religious language works. We must accept that the limits of human existence are beyond human understanding – as St Paul said 'Now we see through a glass darkly, but then face to face' (I Corinthians 13.12). All our explanations are only to reassure ourselves and do not answer anything. Talk of God is actually a mode of acceptance, but not an explanation. Talk of the will of God is again expressing our attitude of acceptance.

✳✳✳✳SUMMARY ✳✳✳✳

● The Irenaean theodicies state that God allows or causes evil as a test for man and that man cannot presume to understand God's purpose.

● The Augustinian theodicies state that man alone is responsible for evil, because of his misuse of the gift of free will.

● Richard Swinburne developed a theodicy suggesting that evil has benefits as a learning tool or can lead to greater good.

● The consequences of evil must follow, or there could be no concept of our responsibility for each other.

● The existence of evil is the cause of many good deeds.

● Natural disasters may still be explained by the Fall of man, as this has affected the whole of creation.

● Ultimately, God has shared our suffering and therefore cannot be accused of inflicting it on us from an aloof position.

Issues for Belief in God Today: Science

Science and religion are widely regarded as being at odds with each other. Wittgenstein would have described them as different 'forms of life', involving different 'language games'. Although rational, scientific language using logic and other scientific/philosophical tools is evident in attempts to prove God's existence and aspects of His nature, many have argued that these attempts fail – whether from Wittgenstein's revisionist viewpoint, or that of the atheist or the believer honest enough to differentiate faith from certainty.

While there is no room here to go into any great detail about the conflicts between religion and science, we will discuss what have been widely regarded as the greatest challenges to belief in God as creator and sustainer: Darwin's Theory of Evolution and the Big Bang Theory. We will look at whether there is in fact any room for reconciliation of religious and scientific beliefs, and at man in the context of scientific discovery. We will examine the question of his rights, duties and boundaries, and the idea of his status as God's steward on earth.

DARWIN AND EVOLUTION

The eighteenth century is known as the Age of Enlightenment and was characterized by giant leaps forward in science. It was an age of optimism and idealism, but without religion's emphasis on a non-material spirituality. It was essentially **humanist**, giving more homage to

> **KEYWORD**
>
> Humanist: philosophical position emphasizing the power of human reason.

nature, which was perceived as an open book providing all answers and equated with reason rather than with God, although He was still seen as its author. By the nineteenth century, nature philosophers were suggesting the inheritance of acquired characteristics and tracing common patterns through, and a unity within, the organic world. Then, in 1859, Charles

Darwin published *The Origin of Species*, which presented a theory of gradual evolution through **natural selection** of the best and most adaptable of each species. This seemed at the time to be in direct opposition to the Christian creation story, where God creates

KEYWORD

Natural selection: theory of the survival of the fittest.

and names each creature out of nothing, and to much religious belief of other traditions, although palaeontology and, later, genetics have shown evolution to be a fact. The theory suggested a world of struggle, where one's own success depended on the failure of others and where moral behaviour might be interpreted as merely a means of preserving one's own species. It may have been this, as much as the apparent removal of God's direct hand from creation, which was felt as a threat to Judaeo-Christian theology.

However, one may argue that there is as much emphasis here on the scope for progress and development in humanity as in many religions. And certainly, to the creationist's protests, one may reply that the Genesis story is no less essentially supportive of their belief if regarded as poetic allegory not to be taken literally, that each 'day' may be taken to represent an 'age' in scientific terms and that evolution need not deny God's place as creator, if His intention in bringing into being the first pieces of matter were that they should develop into their ultimate forms.

It is entirely possible to suspect that many Christians' objections to the theory of evolution were rather to the idea that they could be descended from creatures they regarded as inferior. It might be suggested, from their *own* standpoint, that they insulted God in two ways: firstly, by denigrating any element of His creation as unworthy of connection with man and, secondly, by challenging God's intention and power – there is arguably no reason to see less of a miracle or a divine purpose in the evolution of the Creation than in its springing forth complete.

LET THERE BE LIGHT?

However, many evolutionists certainly did and do not see any possibility of reconciliation with religion. They interpret it as an accidental, chance-based process. In a similar way, the Big Bang Theory is put forward as an explanation of the origin of everything. The theory describes the explosion of a dense mass which then expanded into the universe and continues to expand. But again, if one examines many creation myths, they may easily be read as poetic descriptions of this very type of event – there is little difference in essence between a Big Bang and God saying 'Let there be light' and light suddenly being, in the Judaeo-Christian tradition, although philosophers and scientists would point out that the latter asserts creation out of nothing, while for example dualist Hinduism and the Big Bang Theory have matter existing in its own right, before the universe.

PLAYING GOD

However much scientific belief theists accept, there is no doubt that the advances of science raise many issues of great ethical concern, which have implications for the concept of God as supreme and of man's relationship to Him. There is a saying that if we stand still, we go backwards. Many people, however, are uneasy at the advances being made in our knowledge and will bring forward arguments such as 'we are playing God', 'it's blasphemous', 'we have no right', 'we are destroying God's creation'. Possibly the most well-known complaints of this nature concern genetics, e.g. cloning, genetically modified food etc. Those complaints of religious origin often spring from the Judaeo-Christian and Muslim tradition of man being set as a steward over God's creation, with certain rights, but with inevitable duties also. The ideas we have noted of the *pleroma* (see p. 45), of man working with God, of even having or attaining His likeness and of struggling free from illusion and matter, all involve the acquisition of knowledge and enlightenment. The common thread however is of submissiveness to God, of awareness of His transcendence, or of union with Him as something to strive for, not achievable while in error or bondage to material things. The religious question then is whether man's gift of an enquiring intellect is to be used *ad lib* or within certain bounds and whether knowledge is to be gained for its own sake and the glory of man or to further God's work in man – and how far these are synonymous.

No matter whether a particular religion regards matter as illusory or as a sacred part of creation, life as it is lived on earth involves (for all but total ascetics divorced from the world) a degree of involvement in the material world that is inescapable. Most of us cannot help having concerns about life on earth, whether we believe this is all there is or that it has no ultimate reality and whether or not we believe in a supreme being who is in charge.

With advances in knowledge about the way things work, come added responsibilities and attendant fears about our overstepping the boundaries into what may be seen as God's domain. When we find out how the heart and other organs work, we can soon give people the gift of life by transplants – but attendant concerns are that we may hope for or

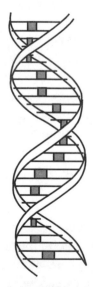

Scientific knowledge of DNA has now enabled us to design it ourselves. Have we the right? Does this make God redundant?

even effect the speedier death of the donor. When we understand about the process of childbearing, we can eventually take away the unborn foetus from a woman if she wishes it – and of course, in some situations, even if she does not – or we can enable someone who is infertile to have a child. Are these advances a natural progression in our growth and development as children of God, working to improve our lives as mirror images of Him, fulfilling His desire for our good? Or are they, as some believe, attempts to set ourselves up to improve on things that God has already ordained?

SUBCREATION

An interesting reconciliation of these two positions is to be found in an essay about the art of the fantasy writer by J.R.R. Tolkien, the Oxford don who wrote *The Lord of the Rings* (1954–5). The idea may be usefully applied to other domains. Tolkien was what would now be called an environmentalist and made no bones about this at every opportunity in his works, seeing the earth as something to be loved and honoured and for which thanks should be given to God. The elements and nature in his books have a spirit of their own which, as well as being a blessing, may rise up against men. Nevertheless, Tolkien saw man as having rights under God as a 'subcreator'. If whatever man did (in the realm of art) were done with reverence for the Creator and in recognition of His supremacy, then his work could be seen as contributing to that Creator's greater work. Tolkien believed that man makes by the law in which he is made and keeps the vestiges of his earlier lordship, although dethroned (by his own Fall). He describes Man as a subcreator, with the single white light of God refracted through him into many colours. Most importantly, reminding us of the free will defence in the last chapter, he said that whatever man chose to do with this subcreative ability, it was his God-given right whether to use or misuse it.

✴ ✴ ✴ ✴ SUMMARY ✴ ✴ ✴ ✴

● Scientific discoveries, such as Darwin's theory of the evolution of species, have been regarded as being in opposition to religious beliefs about creation.

● Darwin's theory threatened notions of morality, in that evolution paints a picture of a struggle for survival, where moral behaviour might be seen as merely preserving one's own species.

● Biblical and other religious texts use symbolic language which does not necessarily conflict with scientific facts.

● The balance between man's rights and man's responsibilities is more and more frequently upset by his scientific and technological advances.

● Man is accused of 'playing God' when he is seen to overstep the boundaries of what is perceived to be God's domain alone.

Issues for Belief in God Today: Theology

With greater communication and greater mobility for the human race comes the phenomenon of the multicultural society. As there is of course not room to trace the theological development of each religion through to the present day, it is proposed to look at theology generally in this current situation and at what various thinkers have suggested in answer to the problem of many faiths all claiming the truth, as well as to societal demands for tolerance and understanding.

PLURALISM

The term **pluralism** may be used to describe either this multifaith society or the particular theological stance taken in relation to it. This stance is that all religions are different expressions of, or paths towards the same essential truth. Possibly one of the best-known exponents of this approach is John Hick (see also p. 9),

> **KEYWORD**
>
> Pluralism: stance that all religions in a multifaith society are different expressions of the same, essential truth.

who suggests that the world religions all have different perceptions and beliefs about and responses to ultimate reality, according to their different cultures and outlooks, but that all are aiming for the same thing – the transformation from self as centre to that ultimate reality as centre.

Of course, the problem here lies in the fact that the difference in these religions' perceptions of ultimate reality is what is central to them and what often makes their adherents choose to believe in them alone as revealed truth. Firstly, culture often constitutes a greater barrier than dogma and it is culture that underpins much of the theology of a religion. Secondly, articles of faith such as the Christian belief in salvation being only through Christ ('I am the way, the truth and the life') can-

not be **relativized** without offence to that religion, so pluralism, which seeks to include all
religions in an attitude of enlightened tolerance, actually denies individual religions validity. According to Hick, the only other alterna-
tives are to say that all religions are false, or

KEYWORD

Relativized: perceived as
not a universal truth, but
applicable only within that
religion.

that only one is true while the others may or may not have elements of
truth, but are inferior. His own view is tempered with the recognition
that no religion can attain to the right representation of the real,
because this cannot be known, and therefore all fail equally but are thus
equally valid. Part of the way in which they fail, according to Hick, is of
course in making claims to exclusive truth! One problem with this
viewpoint is that it still makes (its own) assumptions about 'the Real',
held to be common to all faiths, while at the same time stating that no
assumptions may be held to be exclusively true. Another is that any
specific religion's claims to having revelations of the Real, such as in the

The pluralist and the exclusivist meet head to head. Have they any common ground?

example of Christian salvation, must be rejected because it is held that the Real cannot be known and because no one religion has the truth. This brings the danger of rejecting any such possibility of the Real being revealed or experienced and logically leads to a rejection of all religion, thus defeating one of its own objects – the increase of tolerance and understanding. Gavin D'Costa, an inclusivist, believes that Hick's pluralism is therefore a form of exclusivism.

EXCLUSIVISM

Exclusivism is generally understood to contain an insistence on the **normativeness** (i.e. sole claim to truth) of one's own religion. At its worst, it has resulted in religious wars and persecution (even between different denominations within one faith, as with Catholic and Protestant Christians, or Shi'ite and Sunni Muslims). At its best it dismisses other beliefs as

KEYWORDS

Exclusivism: the insistence on the normativeness of one's own religion.

Normativeness: claiming as the norm, the truth.

error, although it may claim that its own God or reality is open to them. The Protestant theologian Karl Barth (1886–1976) is a proponent of exclusivism, but tempers it with an emphasis on true religion being an inward experience, and all its outward manifestations as being 'unbelief' or merely expressions of desire for control and manipulation. Of course, this has been interpreted as sitting ill with exclusivism and has laid him open to the charge of being in fact a pluralist; his suggestion that another religious believer may be saved whether he knows it or not has also earned him an inclusivist label! (See page 59.)

If an exclusivist's religion teaches any kind of salvation through faith and if it also professes to worship a merciful God, the exclusivist, of course, claiming as he does sole truth for his own religion, must yet reconcile these positions and will often do so by suggesting that the merciful God gives the chance to holders of other beliefs to accept the truth after their death.

INCLUSIVISM

Gavin D'Costa interprets the problem of the pluralism of religions not as being about concepts of and responses to the Real, that vary according to the culture or faith (like Hick), but as the Spirit working differently in different people. Thus culture and individuality are still taken into account, but the difference between religions is the result of particular revelations of the Real at the centre of things, rather than a culture-made one.

Inclusivism takes its stance from within any one religion and believes in the sole claim to truth of that religion, but that others may express aspects of the same and that salvation may not be limited to those sharing the inclusivist's beliefs – even if his religion states that it is! The problem for those who died before the truth of Gavin D'Costa's religion (i.e. Christianity) was manifested, or who for those who have not heard of it, is addressed by the proposition that the former will have a chance after death to hear the 'Word' and the latter will be given the dispensation that their own religion will mediate God's saving grace to them, unless and only until they hear the 'truth' of Christianity. Members of these religions are thus termed 'anonymous Christians'. We can see how offensive this may be to members of other faiths, which also claim, whether exclusively or inclusively, to reveal the truth. D'Costa describes Christ as the normative but not the sole revelation of God. He avoids exclusivism by believing that God's Spirit is active in all contexts and cannot be monopolized by one faith, as this fails to account for the fullness of God's self-disclosure, and by emphasizing what can be learnt from other religions. He equally avoids pluralism by still claiming the normativeness of Christ, i.e. the truth about His person and saving role (although using this as proof of God's desire to save all) and using the Christian Trinity as the model and source of all right action and inspiration.

> ## KEYWORD
>
> Inclusivism: the belief that, although one's own religion is the true one, others may express aspects of the truth and salvation is available to their followers.

* * * *SUMMARY* * * *

- Pluralism describes the situation of a multifaith society, or one of several attitudes towards it. This attitude is that all religions lead to the same truth.

- The problem with pluralism is that each religion believes it alone has the sole truth.

- Exclusivism is the belief that one's own religion has the sole truth. It may be tempered with the belief that members of other faiths still have access to salvation, even without their own awareness, or after their death.

- Inclusivism believes that the Spirit works differently within different people, rather than one's culture determining one's experience of and response to that Spirit.

- The inclusivist states that his own religion has the sole truth, but that this truth will be offered to others in life or after their death.

- Inclusivism states that while one's own faith holds the normative revelation of God, it may not be the sole revelation.

10 Issues for Belief in God Today: Some other -isms

Finally, we shall look briefly at four other issues affecting belief in God today, namely atheism, Marxism, feminism and secularism, and their common emphasis on the human as holding hope for the future.

ATHEISM

An **atheist** believes that God does not exist. There may be many reasons for this belief. Some may be *a priori*, or from reason, e.g. 'I cannot logically believe in the existence of God (whether because I find flaws in the logical proofs for existence, or for some other reason)'. Some may be *a posteriori*, or empirical, e.g. 'Nothing I see around me makes me believe in God' or, more strongly, 'Everything I see around me makes me disbelieve'. Another possible reason is simply the absence of positive belief, e.g. 'If I cannot positively say I believe in God, then I should be honest and say I do not'. This is not to be confused with **agnosticism**, which may describe a lack of certainty about God's existence, or about His nature if He does exist, as well as a questioning of the actual validity of anyone claiming belief or disbelief.

KEYWORDS

Atheist: someone who does not believe in God's existence.

Agnosticism: position of a lack of conviction either way about God's existence.

Of course, many atheists (and agnostics) reach their position after an initial belief in God. They may come to their viewpoint through observation or experience of the evil in the world, and a rejection of the theodicies (see Chapters 6 and 7), through access to scientific data regarded as strong evidence against God's existence, through a change of logical outlook (sometimes occasioned by philosophers who are merely trying to criticize rational proofs, but not necessarily rejecting God), or it may be merely through a rejection of a particular religious upbringing or tradition.

Philosophy, despite such figures as Aquinas and Descartes etc., is usually associated with scepticism in varying degrees, although not all forms of scepticism about God are atheistic. For example, the Dutch philosopher Baruch Spinoza (1632–1677) maintained that God and the Universe were one, which, while rejecting traditional monotheism and the concept of a personal God, does not altogether dispense with the idea of divinity. The seventeenth-century French writer and philosopher Voltaire saw the world as designed, although he did not attribute moral attributes to its designer. Here we come back to the question: What or who is God? Do we mean by 'God' a personal God, or merely a divine essence? May we say that one or the other does not fit with **theism**, merely because it may spring from a different religion or cultural tradition from our own?

Logical positivism, founded in the 1930s, insisted on the verification of all statements and found those about God to be meaningless. However, many atheists do not object to theological language. Many might even claim along with theists that it has meaning in its context and value for human life. We recall Wittgenstein's position here (see p. 35). The

(see p. 35)

KEYWORDS

Theism: a belief in a God.

Logical positivism: theory that only statements that can be analysed through logic are meaningful.

passion against belief in God of one of the most famous atheists, the German poet and philosopher Friedrich Nietzsche (1844–1900), was unequalled. He regarded established Christianity particularly as manipulative and oppressive to the life of humans, because it belittled that life and encouraged a meek 'herd morality', where men do good out of fear and where no one is encouraged to rise above and to glorify man himself. Nietzsche saw morality as smug or, where it involves humility, slavish. Nietzsche's depiction of the death of God is as much a rejection of the religious trap he saw man in as a denial of belief in God's existence and his atheism is as much a revolt against established religion as an intellectual stance.

Some proponents of **existentialism** also allied themselves with atheism, although existentialism originated from the thinking of the Christian writer Søren Kierkegaard. He regarded rational thought about God and His nature as absurd and said that man could only know God through revelation. Because of this, he concentrated on God's existence, rather than His essence or nature. He denied that man was a part of God, as this negated the idea

KEYWORDS

Existentialism: a philosophy that focuses on personal experience and responsibility.

Marxism: theory that human actions and society are determined by economics.

of God existing as a separate and rationally unknowable being. This emphasis on man as free and individual, with the idea of a 'leap of faith' involving loss of preconceptions and an almost irrational commitment, paved the way for the existentialist concentration on the inner life of man and his commitment to himself in what seemed an irrational world. The work of writer and philosopher Jean-Paul Sartre (1905–1980) depicted the pain felt by man at the absence of God, because it is man's nature to believe, and existentialism saw true existence as a brave striving to face up to this absence.

MARXISM

In common with other humanist and atheist philosophies, **Marxism** sought to enfranchise mankind through the development of his awareness of his own worth. Karl Marx (1818–1883) believed man was alienated from himself through the political and economic systems of society and particularly through the religious emphasis on a world beyond and on non-materialistic fulfilment. He famously regarded religion as the 'opium of the people' and advocated a change in man's material situation. He did not object to capitalism in itself, but to a class system which he believed had dispossessed the people.

The seedbed of scepticism and humanism, prepared from the eighteenth and nineteenth centuries on, along with the coming of the Industrial Revolution, which alienated people further from their traditional roots, and the scepticism resulting from the new scientific discoveries we touched on in Chapter 8, meant that Marxism could flourish. It is notable that, while Marxism is anti-religion, it shares with so many religions in falling far short of its ideals in its practice.

Marx, along with Friedrich Engels, followed their contemporary, Feuerbach, in believing that God was not an objective independent reality, but merely a projection of human ideals and of man's nature into something beyond himself, whereas man himself should be the object of religion. Marx saw society as a cause of this error, with man turning from his miserable lot to religion for comfort. He believed it was not enough to recognize the situation, but one must change it and with it the conditions that caused religion to exist and flourish. His vision for society might be likened to the Judaeo-Christian vision of the Kingdom of God on earth.

It is fair to say that theology has been shaken up by those political ideologies in opposition to it and has had to come out of itself and make a response in political, economic and social terms. **Liberation theology**, freeing people in the developing world from oppression and poverty, is an example. The observation that

> **KEYWORD**
>
> Liberation theology: belief that part of Christianity is commitment to change conditions in oppressed societies.

political ideologies claiming to shake off establishment chains and free their adherents have invariably become repressive or bureaucratized regimes themselves may give religions the opportunity to provide the solution, by offering a God who is seen to be *with* His people. Vatican II, with its re-evaluation and liberalization of Catholic dogma and practice, the Worldwide Council of Churches, with its desire for dialogue with other religions, and the Medellin Conference of Bishops, which gave birth to liberation theology, may all be seen as attempts to address the real problems of the modern world.

FEMINISM

The climate of pressure for justice and change has enabled feminism to concern itself with the trappings of religion along with other aspects of society, seeking to gain not only equality of rights for women but a radically altered view of them. This, for the committed feminist, involves a shake-up of religious language and concepts also.

The preponderance of male imagery, let alone the history of male dominance in religion, is regarded as a contributory factor in women's subordinate role. Even such accounts as the Christian Virgin Mary's perceived submissiveness, in accepting God's will for her to be the mother of His Son, is seen as the playing out or depicting of stereotyped gender roles. Some feminists merely advocate a revision of religious writings in the light of a changing world, while others reject them utterly and demand their rewriting. It is not only the religious texts, beliefs, institutional structures and rituals that are challenged by feminists, but the very concepts of God. In Islam, Judaism and Christianity, God is depicted as essentially masculine. Many feminists see this not only as a denial of the obvious female qualities observable in creation, but as a tacit denial of woman's right to be seen as 'made in God's image' and as a reflection of social convention, where man is held to be superior. For these feminists, maleness suggests hierarchy and authority and so they object also to these ideas applied to God, preferring a reciprocal imagery. Much radical feminism does not concentrate on the female to the detriment of others, but seeks a new outlook of equality for all.

Where Christianity is concerned, feminists have objected to the emphasis on Christ's historical person being male and advocate emphasizing rather His message. His death is seen as the result of patriarchal institutions objecting to His inclusive message of justice for all and as symbolizing the death of domination, in being for all a supreme liberation.

Much feminism rejects all established religion as being beyond salvage and advocates new religions such as the Gaia movement, paganism, New Age etc., or the establishment of women's communities divorced

Feminism has rejected traditional patriarchal religion in favour of new alternative religions.

from any religion. Certainly, much of feminist theology and anti-theology has particular links with the earth and uses the pagan images of the mother goddess, with the earth's exploitation and need for healing a part of the larger picture of injustice and division.

SECULARISM

The term **secularism** is used often disparagingly, to describe the decline of both religious belief and outward observance in the modern world. 'Secular' means 'of the world', a opposed to 'sacred'. It should, however, be reiterated that

KEYWORD

Secularism: the perceived decline in religious belief or observance.

the term is often used to describe the decline in overt religious observance, such as church attendance, or in adherence to a traditional, established religion, often a result of today's greater freedom from convention. It need not necessarily be assumed that religion or a sense of the divine is in decline. There are, of course, many opinions on the meaning of the word 'religion' and these will affect how much we can regard secularism as a tendency. Does religion concern 'belief in God' alone, or does it also have an important social and psychological role? If the latter, then secularization involves more than mere decline in traditional religious observance or belief in God.

The term 'secularization' takes different meanings according to whether applied to religion generally or to a specific religion and, if to the latter, whether applied by someone within or outside that religion. If we take 'religion' to mean any activity or ritual that holds meaning, this may still be regarded as secular by those with other priorities. Secularization is, in fact, a cultural as much as a religious concept, in that it is applied differently according to different religious and cultural outlooks and may be applied as much from within one religious outlook to another as from religion generally to what is perceived as non-religious society.

Within Islam, secularization – where intended to mean a decline in observance – is inapplicable, since public worship is inseparable for the Muslim from his inner faith. However, Sunni Muslims might see Shi'ite Muslims as secular because their claim to the right to interpret the Qur'an could be interpreted as accommodating religion to the world and society, breaking with the strict traditions about the divine source of the writing and the censures against its interpretation.

Conservative members of a religion may regard its moves to be seen as anti-racist or anti-sexist as signs of secularization for the same reason – because society is being taken into account, to the detriment of tradition. Even the pluralistic nature of society (see Chapter 9) is a cause of this concern, for adherents to one religion, despite the very fact of interfaith dialogue pointing to a continuing concern with spiritual matters, may see the declining influence of their own religion as a further instance of secularization.

The scientific age and modern social habits are often blamed for a supposedly secular climate and the resulting psychological gap left by the exclusion and rationalization of the **numinous**, but it is noteworthy that in Britain, when a recent Bishop of Durham mirrored the 'age of reason' in his sceptical comments about the Virgin Birth (a basic tenet of the Christian

KEYWORD

Numinous: relating to the divine.

faith), speculation about the subsequent fire damage to York Minster focused heavily on the idea of divine retribution! It seems that, no matter how science and modern attitudes have affected (and secularized) religious ideas, there is still conversely considerable concern about their preservation. Man still has needs that cannot be satisfied by worldly explanations.

It has been suggested by the Romanian scholar and writer Mircia Eliade (1907–1986) that, as secularization in whatever form increases, religion – although less manifest in the public sphere – will become more important privately, with commitment becoming more exceptional but also more distinctive. New religions reach people in a way that mainstream ones are now failing to do. And where religion, of whatever tradition, seems often to have had its function of explaining our world usurped by science, its other function remains the spiritual one of enabling us to cope, of bonding us together, of providing practical rules for life and of giving us a direct experience of the divine, whatever we believe that to be.

✳ ✳ ✳ ✳SUMMARY ✳ ✳ ✳ ✳

- Atheism is the belief that God does not exist, based on reason or experience.

- Agnosticism is doubt about God's existence.

- Scepticism about God need not involve denial of His existence.

- Atheist existentialism concentrates on man's existence and the pain of being without God.

- Marxism sees religion as an opiate and a tool of the ruling classes to keep man in a subordinate position.

- Marxism views belief in God as a misplaced projection of man's ideals, when he himself should be the object of religion.

- Religion has been challenged by such beliefs to meet the needs of modern man.

- Feminism sees religion as perpetuating the subordinate role of women in its male imagery and its hierarchical structure.

- Some feminism advocates rewriting of scriptures; some rejects all established religion as beyond salvage.

- The tendency to secularism is an arguable one, since the term is used very subjectively.

- It may be that religion is merely taking a different direction, rather than being an endangered species.

GLOSSARY

Active Evil The evil that man does.

Advaita Vedanta Hindu term for non-dualism – the idea that all is one, matter is spiritual and there is no division.

Agnostic Lacking certainty about God's existence – literally 'not knowing'.

Anti-realism Denying that something is independent of the mind; in other words, implying that it does not have an independent existence or reality outside our thought.

a posteriori Based on reasoning from facts or particulars back to general principles – literally 'from the subsequent'; inductive.

Apprehension A direct experience or understanding of something through the reason or other means than earthly sight, for Plato a kind of recognition.

a priori Based on reason rather than experience – literally 'from the previous'; deductive.

Archetype The original or prototype of a thing, its perfect example.

Atheism Active lack of belief in God.

Avatar An incarnation.

Circular argument An argument which uses as a proof the very thing it attempts to prove.

Coherence theory of truth That a statement is true if it fits with other statements or outlooks and is in their context.

Correspondence theory of truth That a statement is true if it fits with the observable way the world is.

Cosmological argument Argument for God from the existence of caused things.

Covenant A binding agreement, involving a promise, such as God made with the Jews.

Cyclical Of time; having no beginning or end, continuous, non-linear.

Dualism The belief that matter and spirit are separate.

Dvaita Vedanta Hindu doctrine of dualism.

Eightfold Path Buddhist system of spiritual training that leads to deliverance from suffering.

Eucharist The celebration or re-enactment of the Last Supper, where communion is taken as symbolising or actually invoking God's presence (in the body and blood of Jesus Christ) with the congregation.

Exclusivism The insistence on the normativeness of one's own religion.

Existentialism A philosophy based on the inner situation of man, alone against the world.

The Fall Man's Original sin, and the permanent state of sinfulness resulting from this for all mankind.

Five Pillars The five religious duties of all Muslims.

Formally valid The content or propositions of an argument need not be true to make it a valid argument; if the form is perfect, then the conclusion follows.

Humanist Philosophical position emphasizing the power of human reason.

Icon An image painted or fashioned as an act of worship and used as a focus of meditation, believed to become sacred.

Immanence The quality of being present in all things, so that they are imbued with the divine.

Incarnation The coming of God into the world as man – literally 'in the flesh'.

Inclusivism The belief that, although one's own religion is the true one, others may express aspects of the truth and salvation is available to them.

Infinite regress Where a chain of events or arguments goes back to infinity without a first event or cause as a starting point.

Karma Law of cause and effect governing human existence in which one's deeds govern one's destiny.

Liberation theology Belief that part of Christianity is a commitment to change conditions in oppressed societies.

Linguistics The scientific study of language.

Logical positivism Theory that only statements that can be analyzed through logic are meaningful.

Marxism Theory that human actions and society are determined economics.

Mediator One who goes between, usually concerned with reconciliation.

Messiah The Judaeo-Christian 'Anointed of God', who will come to save his people and introduce a new world order.

Metaphysics To do with ultimate reality, the abstract, the non-material, the transcendent.

Monism The belief that reality has only one basic substance.

Monotheism Belief in one God.

Moral sense The capacity to distinguish virtue from vice, or the admiration felt for good, or a part of the reasoning faculty of man.

Myth A perceived essential truth expressed in story form, with the function of making sense of the world and of man's place in it and his relationship to God.

Natural selection The theory of the survival of the fittest.

Nihilistic Believing in nothing (from *nihil*: nothing); Nietzsche called Christianity nihilistic because he saw it as life-denying, but he is often called a nihilist because he is seen as rejecting moral values.

Nirvana The Buddhist extinction or subsuming of the soul into blessedness.

Normative Claiming sole truth.

Numinous Relating to the divine.

Ontological argument The attempt to prove God's existence through discussion of His nature and necessity.

Pantheism Believing in God as immanent in the material world in a very intimate way, so that all natural phenomena are manifestations of Him, e.g. thunderstorms are signs of His anger, rain of His tears.

Particulars The individual, material realisation of a universal.

Passive evil Evil that is suffered, or that appears to be natural, rather than man-made.

Pleroma The fulfilment of creation, achieved through man's working with God.

Pluralism The situation of a multifaith society, or the attitude that all faiths are paths to the same truth.

Polytheism Belief in several gods.

Predestination The belief that certain of God's people have their fate predetermined and that good works will make no difference.

Redemption Recovery, spiritual salvation through God's sacrifice (Christianity) or mercy.

Reincarnation A cyclical existence of rebirth, returning to life in different forms in order to achieve spiritual perfection or extinction.

Secularism The perceived decline in religious belief or observance.

Symbol Something that stands for something else.

Teleological From the apparent purpose behind the world; to do with goals and completion.

Temporal Of time, rather than eternity.

Transcendence An attribute of God which makes Him above and separate from the material world, beyond the reach or understanding of humanity.

Universals Absolutes, archetypes, the origins of their individual or particular realisations, their referents.

FURTHER READING

General

* *The Concept of God* K Ward, Blackwell, 1974
* *The Puzzle of God* P Vardy, Collins, 1990
* *The Religious Experience of Mankind* Ninian Smart, Fount, 1969
* *The Will to Believe* William James, Dover, 1956

Chapter 1

* *Arguments for the Existence of God* John Hick, Macmillan, 1970
* *An Introduction to the Philosophy of Religion* Brian Davies, OP, 1993
* *An Introduction to the Philosophy of Religion* B R Tilghman, Blackwell, 1994
* *Midwest Studies in Philosophy* Vol 6 P French et al (eds): W D Hudson *The Light Wittgenstein Sheds on Religion*, University of Minnesota Press, 1981
* *The Presumption of Atheism and Other Essays* Anthony Fle, Elek/Pemberton, 1976

Chapter 2

* *The Cambridge Companion to Aristotle* Jonathon Barnes (ed), CUP, 1995
* *Plato & the Republic* Nickolas Pappas, Routedge, 1995
* *The Republic of Plato* Allan Bloom, Basic Books, 1991

Chapters 3 & 4

* *Hinduism: The Sacred Thread in its Continuity & Diversity*, J L Brockington, Edinburgh University Press, 1981
* *How the Churches got to be the way they are* G White, SCM Press, 1990
* *Introduction to Christianity* M J Weaver, Wadsworth, 1984
* *Islam: Its Meaning & Message* K Ahmad (ed), Islamic Council of Europe, 1976
* *A Jewish Theology* Louis Jacobs, Darton, Longman & Todd, 1973
* *Judaism* Hans Kung, SCM Press, 1992

* **Teach Yourself Eastern Philosophy** Mel Thompson, Hodder & Stoughton, 1999
* **Ways to the Centre: Introduction to the World Religions** D L Carmody, Wadsworth, 1989

Chapter 5
* **Myth: Its Meaning & Function in Ancient & Other Cultures** G S Kirk, CUP, 1970
* **The Power of Symbols** F W Dillistone, SCM Press, 1986

Chapters 6 & 7
* **Death & Afterlife: Perspective of World Religions** H Obayashi (ed), Greenwood Press, 1992
* **Problems of Suffering in the Religions of the World** J Bowker, CUP, 1970
* **Reason & Religion C Brown** (ed), Cornell University Press/Royal Institute of Philosophy, 1977

Chapter 8
* **Access to Philosophy: Religion & Science** Mel Thompson, Hodder & Stoughton, 2000
* **Tree & Leaf** J R R Tolkien, Allen & Unwin, 1988

Chapter 9
* **Theology & Religious Pluralism** Gavin D'Costa, Blackwell, 1986
* **Towards a Universal Theology** L Swindler, Orbis

Chapter 10
* **After Patriarchy: Feminist Transformations of World Religions** P M Cooey, W R Eakin, J B McDaniel (eds), Orbis, 1990
* **Basic Beliefs** J E Fairchild (ed): Ernest Nagel, Philosophical Concepts of Atheism, Sheridan House Inc., 1959
* **Religion in Secular Society** B R Wilson, New Thinker's Library, 1966
* **Religion: The Social Context** M B McGuire, Wadsworth, 1987
* **Women & World Religions** D L Carmody, Prentice-Hall, 1988

INDEX

FREUD –
A BEGINNER'S GUIDE

Ruth Berry

Freud – A Beginner's Guide introduces you to the 'father of psychoanalysis' and his work. No need to wrestle with difficult concepts as key ideas are presented in a clear and jargon-free way.

Ruth Berry's informative text explores:

- Freud's background and the times he lived in
- the development of psychoanalysis
- the ideas surrounding Freud's work on the unconscious.

The facts ... the concepts ... the ideas ...

EINSTEIN –
A BEGINNER'S GUIDE

Jim Breithaupt

Einstein – A Beginner's Guide introduces you to the great scientist and his work. No need to wrestle with difficult concepts as key ideas are presented in a clear and jargon-free way.

Jim Breithaupt's lively text:

- presents Einstein's work in historical context
- sets out the experimental evidence in support of Einstein's theories
- takes you through the theory of relativity, in simple terms
- describes the predictions from Einstein's theories on the future of the universe.

The facts … the concepts … the ideas …

JUNG –
A BEGINNER'S GUIDE

Ruth Berry

Jung – A Beginner's Guide introduces you to the 'father of analytical psychology' and his work. No need to wrestle with difficult concepts as key ideas are presented in a clear and jargon-free way.

Ruth Berry's lively text explores:

- Jung's background and the times he lived in
- the development of Jungian analysis in simple terms
- dreams and their interpretation
- classic interpretations of popular myths and legends.

The facts ... the concepts ... the ideas ...

MARX – A BEGINNER'S GUIDE

Gill Hands

Marx – A Beginner's Guide introduces you to the 'father of communism' and his ideas. No need to wrestle with difficult concepts as key themes and ideas are presented in a clear jargon-free way.

Gill Hand's informative text explores:

- Marx's background and the times he lived in
- The ideas that led to revolutions throughout the world
- the place of Marxism after Marx
- Marx's world outlook

The facts … the concepts … the ideas …

SHAKESPEARE –
A BEGINNER'S GUIDE

Roni Jay

Shakespeare – A Beginner's Guide introduces to the great bard and his work. No nccd to wrestle with difficult concepts and ideas are presented in a clear and jargon-free way.

Roni Jay's lively text explores:

- Shakespeare's background and the times he lived in
- the language of the day, clearly explained
- the key themes and elements that have made his work immortal

The facts … the concepts … the ideas …

BUDDHA –
A BEGINNER'S GUIDE

Gillian Stokes

Buddha – A Beginner's Guide introduces you to the Buddha, whose exemplary life and teaching has inspired one of the greatest world faiths.

Gillian Stokes's informative text explores:

- the Buddha's background and the times he lived in
- the legends surrounding this inspirational teacher
- the key teachings and concepts of the Buddhist tradition
- The role of Buddhism in the world today.

The facts … the concepts … the ideas …

DALAI LAMA – A BEGINNER'S GUIDE

Genevieve Blais

Dalai Lama – A Beginner's Guide introduces you to the remarkable story of the man who became leader of the Tibetan people at the age of 4 and who has governed in exile for the past forty years.

Genevieve Blais's fascinating text explores:

- the tradition of the Dalai Lama in Tibet and Buddhism
- the discovery of the 14th incarnation of this spiritual leader
- the historical events surrounding the life of the present Dalai Lama
- the guiding principles and the teachings of this remarkable man.

The facts … the concepts … the ideas …